D0871126

# Mister Raja's Neighborhood

*Letters from Nepal*

JEFF GREENWALD

A JIM COOK EDITION
John Daniel Publisher
SANTA BARBARA
1986

Portions of this book have appeared in
*Connexions, eye, Frank, Metier,*
*Geo, Islands, and Santa Barbara Magazine.*

Maps copyright © 1986 by Michael Pedroni
Cover photo by Jeff Greenwald
Typeset in Garamond by Jim Cook
SANTA BARBARA, CALIFORNIA


LIBRARY OF CONGRESS CATALOGING-IN-PUBLICATION DATA
Greenwald, Jeff, 1954-
Mister Raja's neighborhood.
1. Nepal—Description and travel.
2. Greenwald, Jeff, 1954-   —Journeys—Nepal.
I. Title.   II. Title: Mister Raja's neighborhood.
DS493.53.G74  1986   954.9′6   86-19647
ISBN 0-936784-22-9 (PBK.)


A JIM COOK EDITION
Published by
JOHN DANIEL, PUBLISHER
Post Office Box 21922
Santa Barbara, California 93121

*For every mountain mist,*
*there is a mountain scene.*

—TK

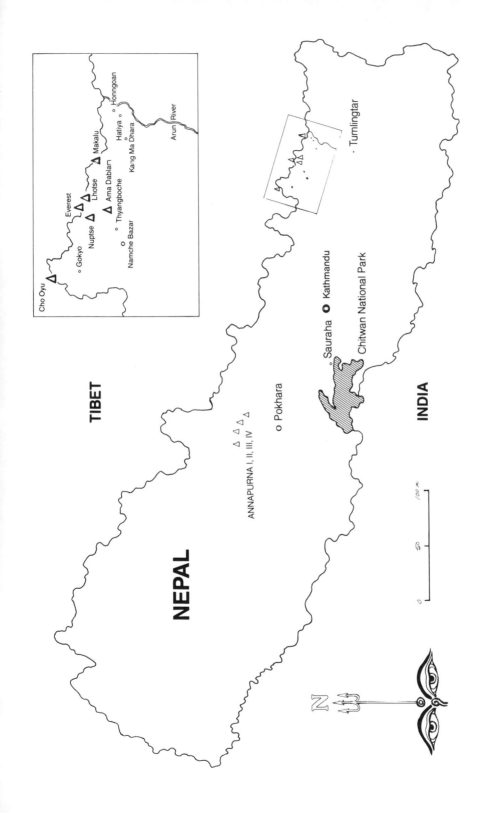

TIBET

NEPAL

INDIA

Cho Oyu

Everest
Gokyo
Nuptse
Lhotse
Makalu
Ama Dablan
Thyangboche
Namche Bazar
Kang Ma Dhara
Hatiya
Honngoan
Arun River

Tumlingtar

ANNAPURNA I, II, III, IV

Pokhara

Sauraha
Kathmandu
Chitwan National Park

0    50    100 Mi.

N

# INTRODUCTION

This book is a distillation of the hundreds of letters and thousands of journal entries I wrote while living in Nepal from June 1983 to July 1984.

Before leaving for Asia I lived in Santa Barbara, working as a freelance writer and graphics artist. My studio was down on State Street, in the old Fithian Building. A lot of artists had their studios there; it was a good time to be working in Santa Barbara. I was publishing *eye,* a portfolio of contemporary art, photography and graphics. David Jekel, my studio-mate, managed the Orange Door Gallery (in the same building) along with our friend Mary Seamster.

Between the magazine, gallery and community of artists, one might think that this was an era of giddy excitement and relentless productivity. Well, sometimes it was. But the truth is that I never felt wholly comfortable in Santa Barbara, "the Versailles of the Pacific." Instead, I was obsessed with the bizarre notion of moving to Kathmandu and working on a novel about Nepal.

This fantasy had been born in 1979 when, after pursuing a particular woman to Nepal, I wound up spending five extraordinary months in the Kingdom. The romance met a gory death, but while in Asia I did manage to write a novel. How this happened was a mystery; somehow, the ambience of Kathmandu ignited flames of both inspiration and discipline in me. It was a state of mind I greatly enjoyed.

Several months after returning to the United States in 1980, I realized that the creative clarity I'd enjoyed in Nepal was fogging. There was nothing to do but plot my escape. The strategy was simple: I would locate an appropriate foundation, engineer an eloquent alibi for dashing back to Asia, and, if it came to an interview, try to present my case without drooling.

It worked. Early in 1983 I received a grant to return to Nepal and "further my skills as a journalist." Although the foundation required no specific project, my strict personal goal was to complete a novel set in modern Kathmandu.

I was certain this would be the easiest thing in the world, and remember yukking it up with my friends: "I'm putting all my eggs in one basket, throwing them 12,000 miles, and hoping that they'll land cooked just the way I like them."

*Bon appetit;* watch out for shells.

# ACKNOWLEDGMENTS

I would like to gratefully acknowledge the friends to whom these letters were written: David Jekel, Mary Seamster, Diana Siegal, Jordan Greenwald, Mom and Dad, Debra Greenwald, Teri Ketchie, Cara Gill-Moore, Edie Moore, Linda Frye Burnham, Brian O'Donoghue, Jim Russell and Carolyn Doty, David McCutchen and Pearl Fisher, Marsea Goldberg, Bobbie Canellos, Jana Canellos, David Rubien, Pat Fish, Nancy Lindborg, Elena Siff, Mike Hoffman, Michael Pedroni, Bill Meessen, Marian Beth Goldman, Amy Gershenfeld, Bonnie Hall, Doug Berenson, Greg Keith, Elaine le Vasseur, David Hacker, Lisa Jarahian. This book is a tribute to the extraordinary rapport we shared.

*

Equally inspiring were the friends with whom I actually lived in Nepal and traveled through Asia. These included people like Elliot Marseille, director of SEVA's blindness program in Nepal; Elliott Higgins, DDS; Peter Westerman; Tomiko Yoda; Ray Rodney; Ambika Kanal; and the unforgettable Howard Sachs, lost to the mountains in the spring of 1984.

Shortly after my arrival in Nepal, Elizabeth Ratcliff invited me to share her lovely house at Nag Pokhari ("Snake Lake"), and from this base many of the early letters were written. On the Everest treks my partner was the indomitable Bill Geary; Brot Coburn, then the UNESCO Alternate Energy Advisor, became a terrific friend and excellent source of information in the Solo Khumbu. Les Iczkovitz and Stephani Lesh met Teri and myself in the Annapurnas, and joined us in Sri Lanka as well.

Teri Ketchie arrived in Asia in October 1983 and stayed until the end of the following March. We traveled together through the Kathmandu Valley, the Himalayas, the Terai jungle, the Indian desert, and around the reefs and mountains of Sri Lanka. Teri brought insight, compassion and a terrific sense of humor to all our voyages, long or short. It is impossible to imagine how dull they would have been without her.

During my final months in Kathmandu I shared a house in the Chhetripaati district with Nancy Lindborg and Rick Gaynor. Chhetripaati is the grinning, dancing skeleton in Hindu iconography, and describes with some accuracy the state all three of us were in by then. In spite of various infirmities it was an inspired time, and generated much of the impetus for *Kanthaka,* my novel-in-progress.

*

The editing of this book was accomplished with lots of help from Alexandra Pitcher, a brilliant writer and true sorceress. Under her sentient eye, a protean mass of letters and journal entries found their most elegant possible shape.

Jim Cook, who first published nine of the (450!) letters from Nepal in *Connexions* magazine, has encouraged this project for over a year—serving as editor, financial consultant, designer, and midwife. Thank you, Jim, for bringing Mr. Raja to life.

NIGHT MOVES ... in a plush living room with the mosquitoes buzzing, the sound of bells outside, always bells even if they're only voices, the dogs that never stop barking, the arrogant horns of the *nouveau-riche*, sound of my own breathing, arrogance of the man alone. Three and a half weeks and already a surfeit of tales to tell. My senses are sharpening to what's going on around here and I'm keeping good company, although none of it stays the night. Only the 'skeeters....

At night, like now, it's usually reflections on what the day wasn't, and sometimes a rare sweet jerk-off to the tune of one of these Newar beauties drawing her sari, all five meters of it, deliciously through my crotch. But there's no point being desperate. Everybody's settled in to their own private safety, and I'm on the waiting list. Come what may, I can't hold on to stateside expectations; everything's drilled at a different calibre here.

Here. What do I see? Gods and clouds reflected in scummy puddles; my own reflection in a bowl of *mo-mo* soup; the brown faces with white teeth and a weird sense of what's funny that I seem to share; the holes burned through my stack of typing paper from the smouldering incense I forgot about; a tree stump hammered thick with ten thousand nails, each one a prayer to the goddess of smallpox; rainbows every evening as the sun breaks under the thick belly of the sky and shoots to where it's been raining.

But it hasn't rained for two days now, and you could cut the air with a *khukuri*. It's impossible to move from point A to point B without a thin scum forming on your body. No amount of the parasite-polluted water can clean you for long. Scratch mosquito bites and worms of dirt roll under your fingers. It won't last long.

I know it doesn't sound very appealing, but the monsoon does have its own peculiar beauty. It's like living in the elbow of a question mark.

\*

Write me a letter and you're in my world, but I know damned well it's a stranger world than any of my friends out there can speculate. We carry sticks to fend off rabid dogs, boil the buffalo milk for twenty minutes before daring to drink it. The flowers that grow here eat human flesh, and all our peanut butter is imported from India. Twice a day the electricity fails, plunging us into darkness or silent light. The nearest ocean is a thousand miles away.

\*

As I came out of Narayan's Pie Shop this evening I saw an odd scene transpiring in the center of the pitch-blacked-out intersection just outside the popular haunt's front door. Someone had built a weird little shrine on the ground, with Indus Valley-esque clay figurines, incense, a burning candle, an offering of cooked rice and about a dozen five-paise coins (one hundred paise in a rupee; one rupee worth about a nickle). It was all right out there, on the scrambled pavement, spared by the wheels of rickshaws and bicycles that hurried by in the otherwise dark. I crept up to have a look, then asked the kid running the "pharmacy" next door was the story was.

"For coots," he said cryptically.

"Coots?"

"No, no, COATS!" He started to laugh. "Like night-time they are coming, bad coats."

Suddenly I understood. Everything in Nepal is understood suddenly, or not at all.

"Ghosts!" I shouted. "You mean ghosts!"

"Yes, yes! Goats!"

We had established that the bizarre construction somehow related to spirits, but any other attempt at drawing the boy out was futile. By the time I glanced back at the shrine a dog had arrived and was gobbling up the rice. The ragged kids came by and stole the coins. A passing rickshaw smashed the figurines. Still, the candle did not go out.

I returned to Narayan's. A Tibetan woman had come in with a wounded crane she's picked up in the street. It wouldn't eat. The bird's wings looked fine, but the eyes held a completely resigned expression. The thing wasn't even fully developed; maybe it had been born sick. I ran next door to the medicine shop, returned with a plastic eye-dropper and showed the Tibetan how to force-feed the crane sugar water. She took over and I left, feeling like a regular *bodhisattva* of compassion.

Rode home through the unimaginable stinks and the hulking shadows of sleeping cows, the racy panic of barking dogs, black alleyways illuminated for blinding instants as gigantic buses heave by, spewing clouds of diesel, black on black, to the posh safety, the rugs and warm lamps and wicker of this house. Sometimes I just want to bolt the door behind me, even though there's nothing and no one to fear. It's an E-ticket ride out there.

JULY 1, 1983
*Kathmandu*

On a tit-shaped hill not far over yonder, Swayambhunath—the Monkey Temple—pokes its white and golden spires toward the sky. I was up there on the 25th, watching the full moon rise over the eastern hills of the valley with a few British and Australian buddies. We sat on the roof of the monastery—the monks couldn't care less—and watched evening clouds roll over the anthropomorphic landscape like the fingers of a masseuse over the Elephant Man's back...lovely, eh? And when the moon finally appeared, a knife in the darkness, the breeze came up and Tibetan incense wafted up from the sacred chambers below...I went from thinking, "This could be the most beautiful place on Earth" to "This *is*." Why, oh why did I have to bring Jeff Greenwald, that notorious workaholic, with me?

# TRAVELS WITH LALJI

I couldn't help but be impressed by the ease with which Lalji entertained his visitors. There were six when I arrived —"Past, present, and potential clients," he later explained. After I'd entered his foyer and taken a seat—an awkward one, higher than the rest—I watched him and listened. His bright eyes, holding the questioners too long; his gift for allegory; things I'd forgotten, or doubted my memory of.

He told a lovely story of a great guru who would not give up his attachment to food. The guru had a voracious appetite, and would often jump up in the middle of discourses to run into the kitchen and see what was being served, and when. "Be still!" his wife would chastise him. "It's your food; no one else will take it. What will people say, seeing you ever jumping up like this? Here you are, a *saddhu*, a holy man, preaching temperance but unable to control your appetite!"

"Dear wife," the guru replied earnestly, "do not worry that I must cling to this one thing; it is in fact all that is holding me to the earth. When you see that I have at last lost my appetite for food, wait; in three days I will be completely gone."

The rest of the story, of course, is obvious—the final confirmation of the yogi's claim. "An enlightened being on the Earth must find an anchor," Lalji said. "Or else he will simply blow away. He is like a man who has climbed to the top of a high, windy peak with an open parachute. The moment he loses his grasp on some earthly thing, he is gone. To take flight from that point—*to actually fly*—is the easiest thing."

Lalji's current forte, of course, is hand analysis, as per the sign in the foyer:

THE LEAF REVEALS THE TREE

THE ROCK REVEALS THE EARTH

THUS THE HAND REVEALS THE PERSON—YOU

His office is quite nice, actually. Bright and austere, enlivened by colorful hand-charts and photograms of hands from fathers, sons, ladies, developing babies.

After the visitors left Lalji's wife brought us tea and peanut brittle. We spoke for several hours about the four years that have elapsed since my last visit to Nepal, when he was holding court at a small chicken farm by the Vishnumati River. Very informal, yet something emerged that I'd quite forgotten; that is, my own peculiar eloquence in Lalji's company. Conversing with the young sage I found myself more concise and expressive than usual, as if his spiritual clarity increased my own, just by proximity. As I described the compromises and triumphs of the past years and my hopes for the current one, I felt I was almost viewing my situation in a new light. Or at least appreciating the balance that I'd struck between my professional and emotive selves.

It was inevitable that our impromptu encounter this afternoon would culminate in an appointment. His wife took over at that point. Painstakingly, almost erotically, she powdered my palms to dry them, dusted them off, and proceeded to apply black ink with a broad roller over every millimeter of my right, then left, palm. She took six impressions, two sets each of the palm, blade and thumb. These she meticulously labeled, and we set up an appointment for next Tuesday. Couldn't help but feel the ball was rolling again. With Lalji to energize me, anything's possible.

JULY 6

Kate and I rode our bicycles together to Lalji's. My continual proselytizing has by now won him several clients . . . Lalji wouldn't see her so directly before my session, so she left her prints while I entered the Inner Sanctum.

Had been bugged by a slight right-brain headache all day, but I felt so relaxed in Lalji's back office that I begged him to proceed. Found out soon enough that his gentle protests actually had a double edge—what emerged after nearly an hour of scrutiny and questioning was that my palms present "an unusual problem." The patterns in both are so similar, claimed Lalji, that he was unable to determine which is the dominant, and therefore could not proceed with the accuracy he felt would be ideal. I was somewhat incredulous; had no idea such a thing was even possible. In a state of amused semi-shock I scheduled another appointment, this one for next Saturday—by which time, hopes Lalji, "things will have sorted themselves out."

So we sat in his reception room for an hour and I explained to him "all about" installation and performance art, calling up as examples Laurie Anderson, Chris Burden, Cristo, Mark Pauline, Mary, Jekel and a few others. He was extremely tickled; not just with the Art/Not Art tales, but by my (unintentionally) funny monologue. When he laughs, Lalji is the very definition of mirth. Wasn't sure I deserved his accolades, but he certainly was enjoying himself.

"I tell you, Jeffrey," he said between gasps, "You are so funny and entertaining that you need never be depressed!" Ah, Lalji! Help me make those words true!

JULY 8

The best parts of today have revolved around cows. The controversy over the dying cow on the Bagmati Bridge is an inspiration to me—the first (published) glimmer of an ecological consciousness evolving in Kathmandu.

Here's the situation: the cow has been lying on the bridge between Kath-mandu and Patan for nearly a week, dying of some unknown ailment while the authorities of both towns throw up their hands and duck responsibility. It takes a sacred cow to bring this out, but the community-at-large is starting to become irate. What's amazing to me is that *the holiness of the cow is never mentioned as an issue*. All the protests have revolved around either humanitarian senti-ment or frustration at the apparent impotence of public officials. I see in this whole pathetic incident a strong glimmer of hope.

And just before coming home, I saw an endearing sight. A cow, just stand-ing bovinely by the entrance to a variety shop. Two Nepalese boys approached. In passing, one of them stopped very briefly to pat the animal on its head and playfully tug her horn. The cow turned its head, poignantly watching the kids go—they hesitated, watching the cow—and then the boy went back, petting the animal some more, whispering pleasantries and finally giving the beast a friendly slap on the rump, at which it cantered off. Life in Kathmandu!

JULY 7 (PALM SUNDAY)

What wasn't picked up by the tape recorder was how the fan whirred bug-green under the intense 250-watt lamp; how I watched the back of the room through the hole in his left ear; how, in between vignettes that he invariably introduced with the words, "Your palm reveals..." Lalji took long sips of water, which he meditatively swished around in his mouth before swallowing, and which borderline disgusted me. Today was the day Lalji read my palms, and although it was a long process and evidently a very well-thought-out one, I just didn't feel (at first impression) that he hit enough nerves to make it worthwhile.

One thing that kept coming up, though, time and time again, was Lalji's warning about how sensitive my physiology is to mental suggestion. And how—as I already knew—this sword cuts both ways. He also stated that this tendency could be easily controlled, with the result of excellent physical health and a long life.

Lalji named crisis and development points in my life's course as well. Thirty to thirty-three, he claimed, will be the major period of "uprooting" for me. "It will be like leaving an asphalted road," he mused, "and entering onto a dirt track—much the kind you would take," he added pointedly, "to reach my house!" Later—toward the end of the three-and-a-half hour session, in fact—I brought up the matter of the novel and asked if he could see an especially auspicious time to begin it. He laughed uproariously, nodding a vigorous affirmative.

"Right now! You should start it right now! Then you can publish it when you are thirty-three! Though you may find it difficult to channel your energies in this uprooted period, it is something, a process, that would be of great interest to others. So by all means, if possible, begin now!"

"You are like a plane on the runway," quoth he, "just preparing to take off."

Lalji also claimed, "by the way," that at fifty-four I'd be at a crisis point in my health, and that some sort of public scandal would ignite and threaten to defame me and damage my reputation. I found this rather flattering, in spite of Lalji's earnest-warning-look. In fact, it seemed like one of the more interesting things to look forward to in a life that will soon, if his predictions are correct, turn markedly inward and become rather solitary. The upcoming stage is the one, presumably, that will culminate in making me well-known enough to be publicly defamed in another twenty-five years.

*

The fact remains that Nepal is a different world, and the edges of Asia scrape incessantly against what's common and true to us-in-America. Even the little things. Drinking tea this morning in the offices of Himalayan Steel, a spry clerk asked me to guess his age. The game never fails to delight the Nepalese. I regarded the man, his eyes alive, his posture erect, hair a distinguished gray above a virtually wrinkle-free face (enlivened by a red *tika*-mark on his forehead) and guessed, charitably, fifty-five. Both he and my translator broke into laughter.

"Guess again."

All right. I guessed sixty-six.

"I'm sorry," my liaison admitted, "But Mr. Manohar here is eighty-four years old."

So many things that are hard to believe; that I'm here at all is a constant source of amazement. Funny how a place can be so much home, yet so full of unexpected angles and inconveniences. A list of things there are not: drinkable water, drinkable milk, washing machines, dish soap, ready telephones, mailboxes, avocados, 35MM slide sleeves, toasters, ten-speeds, size ten tennis shoes, bowling alleys, Dos Equis beer, etc.... but what is here compensates, albeit in a different dimension.

Like the fantastic Swayambhunath temple, high on a hill inhabited by monkeys; I love to go up on full moon nights and watch dusk descend upon the Kathmandu Valley. Since it's the monsoon the cloudscapes are beyond imagining, puffing like huge white blowfish over the towers and pagodas, sometimes running like quicksilver over the shoulders of the hills. From inside the monastery comes the anamelodic rhythm of a *puja* as saffron-clad monks ring thick brass bells and blow through horns shaped from human bone . . . and all around the massive stupa, butter lamps flicker in the breeze.

Night-time is alive and full of mystery. Riding my Hero bicycle over the potted, muddy streets, I catch glimpses of other worlds at every turn. Two men working by the light of a bare bulb, planing huge sheets of wood with primitive hand tools; doorways full of sleeping humans and dogs; the shadow of a sacred cow, shapelessly chewing some rinds thrown out as an offering from a nearby fruitseller. Down the alleys I sometimes glimpse a temple, where vermillion-smeared gods and goddesses dance erotically in the darkness, or where the intense, all-seeing eyes of Buddha peer out with enlightened indifference. Rickshaws, pedestrians and other bikes come bumping out of the blackness at any moment, and only quick swerving cheats a collision.

During the afternoon the sidewalks are a tangled maze of merchandise and humanity where one can find spectacular printed cloth, incense, padlocks, Tibetan *thangkas,* bangles, Yak cigarettes, lentils, sugar, tofu, and tea. Seedy individuals materialize by your shoulder: "Hey, hashish? Heroin? Cocaine? Change money?" Or it'll be some hopeful entrepreneur who reaches into his satchel and extracts a traditional *khukri* knife in a gilded sheath, or a copper prayer-wheel, and waves either or both in front of your face until you break away with an oath and the requisite smile...Grainsellers squat in the stalls alongside huge scales, living on the thinnest profit margin; a grotesque butchery displays the yellow-dyed head of a freshly slaughtered goat, its guts spilled out alluringly below.

*

I wander through my day-to-day, not yet settled, and wonder how the hell I plan to do justice to all this, and how long it's going to take. All my ambitious plans seem so superficial, as if I naively believed I could live in one of Asia's liveliest cities and concentrate only on cuteness. There is a dark side here as well, and it cannot be ignored by anyone who hopes to give more than the tourist-guide impression of the Kingdom. One thing I'm coming to realize: it'll take some time just to sort out what's important and telling and absurd. I can't expect to pull out my pen after one month here and compose a novel that will illuminate the visual extravaganzas, social cosms, religious festivals and cultural avatars of Kathmandu.

# GAJ BIR LAMA

I've been taking a hit or two of weed each day; something I managed to avoid for the first month here. It's a revolutionary act for me in that it throws open the floodgates to all that's involving and awful. For example: one minute I'll be roaring with appreciation at the sight of a thin traffic cop, standing on his little pedestal in the center of a busy intersection, who suddenly drops his whistle and simply gapes in wonder at all the cars around him; the next I'll be gritting my teeth with anxiety, convinced some horrible accident on the crowded, random-motion streets will snap my leg in two.

Then I'll come across a wedding. Fifty beautiful women in iridescent saris parading along, led by a brass band that sounds like it should be practicing in a junior high school bathroom—and within another five minutes I'm waxing philosophical, winding my way expertly through the maze on my Hero bicycle and mentally composing a dissertation on "Subliminal Intuition for Survival Purposes in Fourth World Streets." All this to say, tangentially, that although the novel is still light years from conception, it has indeed begun to form microscopic cells in my brain, and these are beginning the process of division. I needn't mention that even in my driest moments I'm capable of manufacturing excellent possible titles—my favorite so far being "Snake Lake," which is the literal translation of *Nag Pokhari*, the district I'm inhabiting at the moment.

And as the influence of the weed creeps up on me, my ideas come thicker and funnier, the risks seem more inviting, and I can reject the traditional American obsession with heroism and settle for the prospect of being rich and famous.

*

No sooner had I sat down to write than the doorbell rang. I don't remember what I was working on, but I do recall that the interruption was a huge annoyance to me—for when the doorbell rings in Kathmandu, it is not the paper boy or the postman or anyone easily dismissed; it is usually a gratuitous invitation to many minutes of earnest confusion, marked by well-meaning pidgin miscommunication and ending with fruitless dismissal (all smiles, of course); a true diversion of The Flow.

This time things were different. My unexpected visitor was Gaj Bir Lama, a Tibetan artist in his early twenties, who makes his living painting and selling *thangkas*—intricate devotional paintings of Buddhas and other sacred themes. He had brought a few along to show Elizabeth, who was out.

Gaj Bir Lama unrolled the *thangkas*—in this case exquisite portraits of a certain Tibetan saint. I admired the technique; mountains and clouds were built up with points of color, giving parts of the painting a Seurat-like texture. But any resemblance to modern impressionism ends there.

In talking with the artist I learned that Gaj Bir, like his brothers, had studied devotional painting in a monastery in Lhasa, Tibet, for seven years. Each *thangka* was a group effort—his brother would stretch the canvas and chalk in the outlines from rice paper templates; Gaj Bir would then come in with the brush, adding colors ground from lapis, gold, and other minerals. His touch was exquisite, but everything had been done according to rote. With only slight variations, Gaj Bir Lama's paintings resembled those done by his father and grandfather.

I immediately found myself stumbling over questions that seemed both arrogant and painfully American. I inquired if he ever painted strictly "out of his imagination" or "just for fun." Further attempts to determine if Gaj Bir could comprehend "art for art's sake" jarred us headlong into the language barrier, and left me wondering aloud what he would think of my country, "where the art is very, very different."

The encounter threatened to take an absurd tone when I ran off to fetch my portfolio of slides. But I stopped short to consider how I could possibly explain my own *modus operandi*—screwing together semi-random found objects into savvy little collages—to someone who had studied meditative pointillism since the age of twelve.

JULY 20

Details, details. My barber touching the razor to his forehead before beginning.

"Why did you do that?"

"Why? Why?"

"Yes, why do you touch razor to head?"

"Oh. Yes, every time, touching."

"But *why*? For God? For luck?"

"Yes ... luck ... today, you see, you are my first customer."

My original theory was that it was some kind of prayer to prevent himself from inadvertently cutting my throat.

The Prince Barber Shop is a tiny place, but I always enjoy going there. It's painted this unspeakably garish mint-green that seems to be rampant in these parts, as if some company had fifty-thousand gallons of hideous stuff they needed to write off of their taxes and managed to do so by making a charitable donation to Nepali development. It's another of seemingly infinite proofs that the Nepalese can live with anything.

The mirrors break up the space, but I usually spend my time looking at the postcard of Indian starlets he's got jammed into their corners. They're very lovely. One especially, with long hair and doe-brown bedroom eyes. And he's got some ghastly photographs of his own children. The two daughters look fine, but the shots of his son alarm me. No doubt it's some cosmetic improvement by local standards, but he's got the poor kid's hair up in a big bow, and his eyes are totally ringed in thick, black eye shadow. It's like looking at a picture of the eight-year-old Valentino as a vampire. To complete the effect, he's dressed in a white shirt with bow tie and suspender-shorts which appear, in the photo's glossy gleam, to have been tailored out of plastic. It's clear who the "Prince" is....

JULY 21

As far as the novel goes, if my final task is to create an exotic and delectable omelette, I'm just at the point where I'm shopping around for hens. (The house I'm staying at now has a chicken—her name is Kumari, and I have this recurring nightmare she's actually a legal secretary trapped in the body of a domestic fowl. Every time I start to type she's up on the windowsill, chattering away as if to criticize my tedious hunt-and-[no pun intended] peck.)

Today Elizabeth is sick, and I am faced with the necessity of taking over the class she teaches at the English Language Institute. I taught there last time I lived here; this time I don't think a steady job will be necessary. But for the afternoon I can look forward to teaching a bunch of twenty illiterate Sherpas such timeless expressions as, "How would you like your hamburger, sahib," and, "Sir, there is a leech on your ass."

I've never seen a storm like it. The sky is white with lightning, and the tempest shows no sign of abating. I sit here in my little flat—a monsoon sublet—in a violet and turquoise *lungi* and feel what tobacco's done to the back of my throat. My hair is soaked.... Peter and I just rode our bicycles home from the downtown area, fed up with waiting out a storm that's obviously just getting its claws out. (The lights flicker. For a moment the frantic strings of Rachmaninoff's *Rhapsody on a Theme of Paganini* are slowed. I'm well prepared; soon as I got in, after taking off my sopping clothes, I shoved about half a dozen candles into their brass or clay holders. Even though loss of electricity is as common as cowshit here, it never fails to raise my hackles). It was a terrifying experience, as I recounted to him tales of various acquaintances who have lost their limbs to lightning. We made it though, I praying to the One True God as the sky panicked into pink and blue and cream and the houses and huts stood out broad as daylight...fearless rickshaw drivers heaved by in the downpour, grinning and nodding with the inevitable, "Hello, rickshaw?" Couples of men and men—and women and women—scurried past with their arms around each other, sharing umbrellas. The Year of Living Damply. I don't look a bit like Mel Gibson, even soaking wet.

Today was a red-letter day for me; began my intensive Nepali reading and writing course. Six hours a day, plus homework, for the next two weeks, then off to a backwoods village to cement it in. It's a holy terror and a terrific pleasure to be on the other side of a chalkboard after having taught English here...My teachers are Nepalese, the classes are lively and small, and I'm no dumber than anyone else. One of the peak experiences of my life occurred at 11:30 A.M. this morn as I wrote my first word in *devanagari* script. It means "lotus"; the word is pronounced *kamala*. You'd be amazed how quickly I'm picking up the writing end of it...maybe I've got a special propensity for symbolic ciphers, et al. As far as the spoken language, my position in the practice dialogs has been best described by Gauguin: "The Devil would be better off in a holy water basin." But it'll come with time.

Learning Nepali—and especially devanagari—has been, is being, an amazingly rich experience. The first week ended today. It's been all-consuming; the time I'm left with afterward is fit for sleeping, eating, postulating. Little else. Every once in a while something will come along and kick your ass and remind you what hard work thinking can be. It's like working out, pulling up from atrophy that part of your brain that constructs cohesive systems from disparate parts.

Incredible how much about language we take for granted—the deep structure is quite beyond me, but even simple gestalts (*e.g.,* the present-tense conjugation of the verb "to be"—*ho*) require enormous expenditures of real energy to master. If there were muscles up there, they'd ache.

It's especially fascinating to me because, since 1971, I've wondered how it would feel to look at a printed page without having sounds and images impress themselves upon my consciousness. Meaning it's impossible to glance even for a microsecond at the word "cat" without saying it in your brain and receiving a cognitive picture of a cat form. Last visit, in 1979, I experienced that ability, so to speak; I could look at a page of devanagari script with zero comprehension. But for the past week I've been re-awakened to the childhood experience of learning a completely new alphabet. First sounds; then words; and finally words with comprehension. It's truly a thrill.

AUGUST 8

Odd holidays. Yesterday the little kids were out in the streets with rude roadblocks made of string, spit, and tin cans. Demanded *paisse* from passersby. The taxis and foreign-aid mobiles ran right through the pathetic barriers, often almost jerking the kids' arms along with them. If I'd tried to on my cycle I would have been decapitated. "Mister," this one little kid explained, "this is *very good* holiday for us. You must pay." "Hunh?" "This is our *very good* holiday. You give us some *paisse* so we can burn the ghosts tonight. Down by the river, all the ghosts burning." Those ghosts again. Who can argue with this kind of talk? I gave the kids twenty *paisse*—four coins worth, cumulatively, about one cent—and they let me through. Next day I read it in the paper; it was legit. Another Invisible World.

\*

Another scene: Friend Peter stops his bicycle and waits for me to catch up.
"Man, you'll never guess what happened to me two nights ago."
"You're right."
"I was just laying in bed, reading . . . and all of a sudden I shit in my pants!"

\*

French women and hashish. My own lonesome fears and the eternal womb of the mosquito net. "Learn to love being sick." Outside the lightning flashes and dogs howl and some Nepalese man walks down the hair's-breadth dirt road singing at the top of his lungs. It's midnight. The rats have quit the kitchen. Lizards scurry across the walls, never missing their prey.

AUGUST 9

'Fraid it's going to be catch-as-catch-can with this letter; it's 7:30 A.M. and I just woke up from a night of bizarre dreams that I've already mostly forgotten. Woke up wondering where the hell and I was and not too damned pleased to find out. All night it poured; I lay in bed with a hard-on. By five the neighborhood Nepalese were up and about making an extraordinary amount of noise even for a Saturday. You don't hear Nepali kids cry much, but when they do nothing can top them; there was one babe this morn who raised the practice of shrieking to an art. When he/she was finished a taxi pulled up somewhere nearby. As the children, so the horns; this *mullah*'s instrument sounding like a beached elephant seal, and he *leaned* on it. That got me up. Another minute and I would have stunned the locals by ripping the thing out of his car. Ah well! All these aural idiocyncracies might be tolerable if not for the fact that the woman who subletted me this flat (she's in England for the monsoon) failed somehow to mention that it's within shouting distance of the infamous Copper Floor Disco, Kathmandu's only all-night disco. And last night was Friday.

*

AUGUST 10

Today being Saturday, I decided to explore...took the motorscooter a friend gave me and headed up to Bhaktapur, which used to be the artisan's center of the Valley. Arrived at 8 A.M. to a sight that took my breath away: off to the east, the north, the west, steel blue peaks thrust above the clouds and gleamed in the morning light. The Himals are incredibly young, and *sharp*. Seeing them like that, so high, so much by surprise, filled me with a longing that I've experienced only in a sexual way before. I wanted to possess those mountains, to penetrate every angle and swell of them. To get out of the soiled Kathmandu Valley and into the Eternal Winter, out onto those staggering peaks. Unlike any other range I've seen, the Himalayas exert a pull that's actually felt inside the body, as if iron filings had been injected into one's blood and huge magnets placed on the horizon. Soon enough—October at the latest—I'll be journeying out that way. Those are the experiences that change you.

AUGUST 17

In his bright yellow cotton shirt, amber-rimmed sunglasses and purse-lipped delicate elegance, Bhushan Lakandri—star of the recent *Ramayana* production —looked every inch a late-sixties era faggot. Truth or illusion? Why do those perfect Indian features, those proportions of deity, invariably look effeminate? Ah, pitiful western man. In the East, you see, they never needed to rub their own noses in the contrast between how masculine men look and how feminine women...In addition, could it be that the human face at its most gentle, and/or most godlike, does indeed tend toward female? No mythic Garden of Eden here, to caste the sexes in opposite corners; in Asia the roles are shared. Rama, Durga, Ravana, Shiva, Parvati; the in and out of things.

But it's funny—Bhushan would have looked even more feminine *if he had not been holding that bunch of flowers.* Something about the authority with which he held them; with which only men hold flowers and babies. An authority with tendrils in both appreciation and intimidation.

And he held my hand. When we were introduced; held it for such a long time that, again, I had to let my mind slip into a different way of perceiving affection. That simple *taking* of the hand, without the need to shake it, squeeze it, even grip it—and as I ended my first thirty or forty seconds with the actor I realized that, while as an American man I can shake hands as good as anybody, here in the East I am lost at sea in the non-aggressive, undefensive palm of Rama-cum-Vishnu-cum-Bhushan.

AUGUST 24

I'm sitting here in my blacked-out living room with a saffron string tied around my wrist (a Brahmin put it there yesterday morning on the auspicious occasion of *Janai Purni*, and there it will remain until *Laxmi Puja* in November, when I and every other bestringed fellow will clip it off and attempt to affix it to the tail of a sacred cow...) and a very pink case of conjunctivitis in my eyeballs. Pus occasionally drips onto my lap, but I demurely mop it off. One gets used to all manner of grossnesses here, although, as a number of us were discussing at dinner the other evening, there are *some* things you never can take in stride. I'll save them for the next time *we* have dinner together.

# DAKSHINKALI

I'm in an experiential mode, letting ideas—and contracts—accumulate. Certain at this point I'll be here more than a year, and trying to set some reasonable goals. New first-year plans: to get a respectable grip on the language; to outline some major novel-possibility themes; to write and publish four major magazine articles.

The novel business is a funny thing because it combines so many things—internal and external needs that are important to me. It's an obsessive idea in its current state, though, representing solely ambition rather than expression. What I mean is, when I have something I need to write about, I'll write it. Meanwhile I'm going to try to relax. Snatches of dialog, scene changes pass through my head like clouds...sometimes erotic, sometimes horrific, sometimes satiric.

Every Saturday, my friend Peter Westerman and I head out of the city and attempt "cultural satori" by journeying to spots of interest, ritual, and/or enlightenment around the Valley. Last Saturday, for spontaneous reasons that mysteriously over-rode many past trepidations, we took the morning bus eighteen kilometers south to Dakshinkali.

Dakshinkali, or "southern shrine of Kali," is where the Hindu goes on auspicious Saturdays and Tuesdays to make a wish, to ask a favor large or small from that particular goddess. Ah, but everything has a price...for Kali/Durga is the goddess of wrath and destruction, and in order to petition her one must make an offering of some sort. And there's only one sort she'll accept: blood.

The bus wasn't as cramped as some I've been on—my groin grinding against the round, virginal ass of an otherwise unapproachable Nepali sylph—but the lack of human company was compensated for with a preponderance of goats and chickens, all marked on the head with red *tika* powder. Outwardly calm, the goats farted incessantly. Ever smelled a goat fart? At any rate, we all petted and "made nice" to the animals, for they were to be greatly honored, and destined to bring great luck to their households.

Uphill all the way. Miraculously, the monsoon clouds had drawn back a fraction, and we could see the impossibly high flanks of the northern Himals rising from beyond the valley wall. A sight to make your heart leap...nothing on Earth compares, literally as well as spiritually. We crested the ridge after Chobar Gorge (sliced from the mountain by the sword of Manjusri when, thousands of years ago, he drained the valley of water and exiled the proud Snake Kings) and cross-backed down to a parking lot full of other buses. Ours—and the others—would wait an hour, then return the cargo of people-minus-animals to Kathmandu.

The air was thick with smoke, and rancid with the odor of boiling flesh and fresh blood. Along the river, beneath a maze-like confluence of bridges full of gorgeously dressed women and solemn men waiting their turns, squatting pockets of men scooped entrails out of decapitated goat bodies and washed the whitened viscera in the clouded water. Peter and I descended to the area where the separate queues of men and women converged. The area—leading into the open-air but enclosed sacrificial arena—was densely packed with devotees and tourists, and I couldn't see a thing. But patience won out...after hanging around a bit I found myself pressed against the metal bars, telephoto in hand, staring with fascinated revulsion at the stone idols utterly bathed in thick crimson, at the tiled floor-area ankle-deep, at the smiling women with flowers and incense and saris and blood-spattered feet. Still couldn't see anything, as the inner-sanctum Hindus were gathered around the decapitating altar. Most of the killings are done with one, quick stroke, and it's considered bad luck if the head is not severed at once.

As I stood there, two men, obviously the "executioners," led an unresisting goat onto the spot not six feet in front of my face where the gruesomely abluted idols of Kali and Ganesha waited expectantly. They sprinkled holy water on the animal's neck, scratched it with deceptively gentle fingers, grabbed it under the legs, pulled its head back and...

I was fine while I snapped the photos. Caught the first few slices, the blood spurting onto the deities, the continued struggles and final result, the headless body kicking on the ground. Snap, snap, snap. Then I backed away, and as my lungs filled with the foul, thick smoke and awful smells, I fell onto a bench. My ears were ringing, and I felt the blood draining from my face. Every pore opened and I found myself instantly drenched with sweat. My vision began to blur, too, and, realizing to my horror that I was going to faint, I plunged my head down between my knees and tried to breath deeply and evenly. It worked, thank God—fainting at Dakshinkali would have been a pretty humiliating experience, even though I'm certain it's happened before. But the fact remains that I was affected in a profoundly physical way, and even now the memory of what I saw there fills me with loathing. You go through your life here, dodging trucks, smiling at the monks with quartz watches, stopping in front of the import stores to see the selection of cassettes, and you forget what a thin veneer the western influence has pasted over what is basically a very superstitious, pagan society. It makes me think neither more nor less of the Nepalese, but it sure opens my eyes as to where I really am. This is *not* Middle Earth.

SEPTEMBER 1

Nepal. Bracing itself for the tourist onslaught. The mountains still hidden beyond the Valley rim, but within another month they'll be out, glistening on the horizon like salt crystals on a margarita glass. Lazy as ever, I spend most of my days jetting around town on my red Bajaj scooter, running errands and trying to neatly set up the upcoming months, like a row of dominoes, so that when I finally do get my ass in gear things will simply move along with all the effortless efficacy of a chain reaction. At present I feel rather like a highly sophisticated machine with an essential and simple part missing—passion. There's still very little of it in my life right now, and none at all of a sexual nature. I'm thrilled to be here, and amazed by what I see and contrive—the humorous situations, the absurd interface between East and West ("the only thing melting is the pot"), the grisly local attractions ranging from live animal sacrifices to hospital scenes I wouldn't want to describe. There's a gulf, I'm finding, between being in a mentally assailing environment and being able to sort out that environment into literary vignettes. One thing I've got to teach myself is how to think *small*. If I'm shooting for the Great Asian-American Novel, I'll never get started. Like so much else it's a matter of focus. And of learning. Ten weeks in, but I'm still green around here. So much I'm trying to understand; so much that reveals itself only slowly.

Tonight is Krishna's birthday; as I sit here typing I hear a riot of drums and flutes and cockeyed horns parading past the gate, and jump up to check. A stream of people filter by, trodding barefoot through the muddy lane, their faces lit by the white glow of kerosene lamps and fat candles. Smoke rises into the carbon-black sky. Four of the men carry a lively palanquin, upon which sits a tiny idol—the image is so bedecked with flowers that it's impossible to make out the blue-faced Krishna within. Ah, the autumn...from now on, the festivals come hot and heavy. Last week was *Gai Jatra*, day of the procession of the sacred cows, when every family who lost a loved one during the past year hired a cow, bedecked it again with flowers, and led it through the streets...the wealthier families also had crazily garbed bands with them. All the bereaved families (though you never would have guessed it by looking at them) with sons went a step further—the boys were made up to look like cows, too, as well as kings and *saddhus* (holy men). The theory is that honoring a cow in such a way will entice a sacred bovine to accompany a dead spirit as it makes the treacherous journey toward the gates of Yama, across the Rivers of Fire... these people *invented* performance art. Can you imagine the scene? The streets packed with people and drunken musicians as hundreds of mourning families parade through the streets like Halloween, cows in flowered necklaces everywhere, ten-year-old Nepali kids with pasted-on paper beards and canes hobbling beside them...what a world. From *Laxmi Puja* to Laurie Anderson, I love it all. And coming up next week is *Teej*, the women's festival, when all the females in the valley dress in brilliant red shirts, saris, and dresses, and make a mass pilgrimage to the holy Bagmati River (which, a few hundred kilometers south, is called the Ganges). They strip and bathe erotically in the fast-moving waters, praying to Shiva for their husbands' virility, while the men themselves watch gleefully, often with binoculars, from the opposite bank.

SEPTEMBER 5

The American Compound, bunch of tight-assed Development Brahmins, occasionally surprise even themselves by bringing some pretty good films to town. Mostly I stay home, not actually being allowed to enter the compound and needing a member to escort me. Also I've seen nearly all of the junk they import: *Private Benjamin, The Shootist,* etc. You know, C-grade stuff. Last night, though, I couldn't resist. Asked friend Elizabeth to take me out and, though she walked out after about fifteen minutes, I finally saw *The Road Warrior.* Gave me weird-ass nightmares, that's for sure. The culture-shock was amazing. Came out of the auditorium, mounted my deadly Bajaj scooter (more powerful than a starving *saddhu*) and roared off into the diesel night, ready to kick the shit out of any rickshaw-*walla* that got in my path.

OCTOBER 11

A lazy Monday afternoon, spent running errands and trying to prepare for my upcoming short-but-important trip to India. I'll probably be there by the time you get this letter; hoping to leave the 20th or so. This trip, of course, for the GEO story. A lot is riding on it, and I'm trying to approach it with as many advantages as possible. So today I went to the Indian Embassy for a letter of introduction, tried in vain to get my passport back early from the Foreign Ministry (they're processing my residential visa), and searched in vain for a tube of tasty Vajradanti (literally "lightning-tooth") toothpaste to replace my boring and nearly depleted Dolomite health-food paste. Even in Nepal—or especially in Nepal—I can't tolerate the thought of bland toothpaste.

The days aren't all so sensational, but they are all full of contrast. It's all a matter of degree, but I definitely seek out the realms of shock and difference. An afternoon hike to various shrines hidden atop valley ridges might be followed by a dinner with some secretive gold-smugglers; a dinner of *dhalbaat, mo-mos,* and *tarkaari* might be completed with apple pie à la mode. A friend and I toast each other with Cokes, and simultaneously swallow our deworming pills. Despite the garrulous industrialization of Kathmandu, it's impossible to forget you're in Nepal.

Rosh Hashana passed without much fanfare here; the half-dozen Jews I know were marginally aware of it, but it was an ordinary day for most. As for myself...well, I guess you could say I had a "religious experience" of sorts. That particular day my classified ad came out in the *Rising Nepal*: Writer seeks bright, airy flat, etc., and I spent a lot of time chasing down responses.

Late in the day, after I'd more or less made my decision, I decided to visit one last place. Walked in and found myself standing smack in the middle of a Star of David inlaid in the stone floor. (That, as well as the swastika, are the most commonly seen good-luck symbols in Nepal...both derive from Sanskrit traditions.) Needless to say, the place was the best one I'd seen all day, and I took it at once.

*

Gearing up for India. Seeking visas, letters, tickets. I've got the strongest confidence in this assignment—seems like any problems that arise will come from too much information rather than too little. There's no doubt this is the door. Without panic or ceremony, I plan to simply open it.

SEPTEMBER 16

Removing one's props leads to boredom; later to contemplation. I sit here in the studio listening to the crickets outside (and inside; there's one in my typewriter case) and wonder what I have to discuss with God. *Erev Yom Kippur:* tomorrow the Book opens, and my name is in it. "Who by rabies, and who by dysentery..." My fingers are crossed.

Reviewing the past year in my mind, the sins do not seem to merit capital punishment. In fact, what I have been guilty of most of all is being a clumsy Jew. "The emptiness of neither believing nor not believing in God," writes Rushdie in *Midnight's Children.* But I do believe in God, I do, I do, and also believe in the (sort of) religious doctrine espoused between-the-lines by Rushdie: that faith heals, each cure according to its kind, so be careful of what you choose to believe in out of the zillion choices....

Guilty of arrogance. Guilty of laziness. Guilty of boasting. Guilty of gossiping. Guilty of lust. Guilty of hatred. Guilty of not returning love. Guilty of not loving myself. Guilty of enjoying graven images. Guilty of jerking off too much. No need to play the flip side; my *mitzvahs,* hopefully, will strike a balance, slightly skewed in my favor, and set me up for another year of baffled perseverance.

Personal questions about God and my own purpose have been bobbing at sea for years now. Gone, except occasionally, the bursts of absolute self-confidence and convictions of inspirational virility, which always tracked back to love of God. These days I seek a bridge that will allow me to *puja* Ganesh with impunity, yet maintain the great fury of Abraham from bursting my skull. I might as well try grafting avocados onto a pine tree; the rules laid out are sometimes pretty damned clear.

The current predicament is necessary but unsatisfying. I have my roots, but

I'm up in the tree. And while I'm on the one hand obsessed with providing myself that grass-roots nourishment, how can I help but want to just sit back and enjoy the view?

*

The upcoming stories that I'm doing—the Caves of Ellora for *Geo,* and Sri Lanka for *Islands*—have me in an excited and curious state. In a way, they'll work pretty strongly to determine my future course. *Geo* has assured me that if the Ellora story impresses them there'll be more work for me. What I'm looking for is the ability to write these critical "introductory" articles without being cowed. To write with humor, sentience, and confidence. Well, this coming Sunday I'll be off to India on the first of the assignments. Wish me luck.

Today and yesterday were red-letter days. Something in the weather broke, and a kind of clarity defined the air. The energy-depleting days of steamy heat and intermittent downpours seem to be ending. Suspense fills every glance at the valley rim as we wait for the icy Himalayas to reveal themselves at last. The valley is large and very open, but when the monsoon clouds lift and the mountains rise incredibly in the not-so-distant north it fills one's soul with an animal magnetism unlike anything else I've experienced. Did you ever watch a cat watching a bird from behind a screen? They make a funny baa-ing sound, a psalm of primal longing. That's how my spirit feels when the Himalayas catch the evening light. The magnetism that drew me, and is drawing Teri, out to Asia is indigenous to the area. I'm its most humble regent, nothing more.

# ELLORA REFLECTIONS

The globe, the globe. Glowing gobules. Pulsing papules. Infectious hepatitis, mutual orgasm, the Wheel, *masala dosas,* and myths . . . let me tell you, India is quite a place. Got back at two this afternoon, after a brief stopover in New Delhi that capped off a five-day journey to the outer and inner edges of awe. There are a lot of old temples in India, and all of them are beautiful, but the stone-hewed caves of Ellora and the ancient, brilliant murals of Ajanta take all for mystery, eroticism, and humor.

Ellora was my assignment. I'd been there once before, for a single day, in 1979; that had been a spontaneous sidetrip and I'd figured, "Caves, big deal, no use taking an extra roll of film along. . . ." Jeez, was I in for a surprise. Well, I was finally able to make up for that fiasco.

Ellora! Cave-temples carved from a basalt cliff between AD 600 and 1200; monuments to the three great faiths of that span (Buddhism, Hinduism, and Jainism) and an even more impressive testament to the days when the prime directive of a king—any king in India—was to encourage the religious spirit of his subjects, whatever form that spirit might take. That six-hundred-year period in Indian history witnessed two enlightened dynasties, patrons-of-the-arts extraordinary; I witnessed the eternal evidence of their beneficence.

There are about fifty caves in all. Some stretch across the broken cliffside, punctuated by waterfalls and joined by rough stairways. Others are grouped less formally above the butte, ringing with sylvan rhythms at the headwaters of the falls. Mysterious places where stone pillars reverberate like tablas; deep worship-caves as cavernous as cathedrals; galleries of gods and goddesses frozen-yet-not-frozen in scenes of heroism, dance, erotic love. In some caves, little islands of color indicate that the caves were once painted with lively celestial scenes, like their earlier companions at Ajanta; but I'll get to that.

The Hindu caves really burst into life, bristling with eroticism, power, and terror. Dedicated exclusively to Shiva, they portray the deities with an intimacy and humor that is entirely unusual. I stood in awe before the worn, pitted panels, understanding for the first time that the smaller figures in the friezes may have been so rendered to lend *perspective.* Shiva and Parvati in their adorable dice games; the Lord of the Dance; the obscenely mischievous *ganas* and patient, baffled-looking Nandi, victim of their pranks. It seemed to me that the Hindu artists may actually have been inspired (or at least egged on) by the pure sobriety of their Buddhist counterparts. Still, the impression I received overall was definitely of artists-in-cahoots. It couldn't have happened any other way.

Of all the caves, the most spectacular is inarguably Kailasa. According to

Hindu mythology, Kailasa is the Himalayan home of Lord Shiva, the balancer of destruction/creation, Master of the Dance. Graced by the voluptuous Parvati; shaken by Ravana; it remains a wonder of the world.

Sadly, the paintings that once covered the great temple have worn away and been scratched out by grafitti. Only stone abides; and that too is disintegrating. In two hundred, three hundred, one thousand years, there'll be nothing left. The tragedy of this is sharply focused when you consider that it took over seven thousand artists at least thirty years to carve, from the top down, this faithful model of Kailasa from the live stone at Ellora. Three million cubic feet of basalt were taken out, but nothing was brought in... every hallway, pillar, sculpture gallery and stairway was brought down from what originally existed, an ancient echo of Michelangelo's contention that the forms are already there, waiting to be released from the primal stone. The excavation is nearly a hundred feet deep, and with a little bit of climbing you can stand on the shoulder just above it, looking down into the teeming chasm and trying to convince yourself that the thing really does exist.

And this is just one of the caves.

All week I found myself running into religious guilt vs. when-in-Rome enthusiasm. Felt too close to Yom Kippur to begin worshiping local gods. But I had nothing against chanting in the high-domed Buddhist enclaves, or attempting to draw sexual power from the Shiva lingam (*i.e.,* phallus) in Cave 15. As I loosened my collar and called upon Yahweh to forgive me if this wasn't really His Wang, my voice echoed through the stone vestibule and sounded like a richly blown tuba.

The assignment was defined by auspicious meetings. Deva Vasanthroa is a pensive-looking pen-and-ink artist who has haunted the Ellora Caves for months. He never took off his corduroy hat. I interviewed him for a while, but he was tongue-tied and I finally had to agree with his apology: "A person like me, around these monuments—even if I say more, it is less."

During our first meeting we spent over an hour strolling the lush, slippery path between the later Hindu caves. Deva revealed many aspects of the scenes that would have escaped me otherwise: how the *ganas* taunted Nandi and bit his tail; how Shiva sat with his hand gripping Parvati's sari as she tried to rise after beating him at dice ("If a man holds a woman that way, she cannot leave with her modesty"); how certain cuts were made in the stone to allow more light in. How a tourist plunged to his death last year trying to jump across the high, spouting waterfall.

*

Woke after a fitful night's sleep to a morning of lightning bolts and rain. No sun, and the fog hanging dense over the hillocks. The power blacked out as I shat; determined to make the best of a bad situation I threw on my parka and wandered out in the rain toward the Buddhist caves. My hope was to hear thunder echoing through the stone halls, but by the time I arrived in Cave 10's spooky sanctum the only things audible were thin streams of water running down the cliffs and the weepy radar of confused bats.

One of yesterday's highlights was the hike I took with Deva. Starting at the paved roadway we made our way out to the Jain caves. Along the road Deva searched for a strong, straight twig he could whittle down into a holder for his pen-nib. We cut an unlikely pair: I with my "Mid-Island Y" T-shirt, harnessed by camera gear; he in the perpetual corduroy hat, holding a double-edged razor blade lightly between his fingers.

As we approached the small, semi-circular grouping we came upon two khaki-clad men lounging beneath a tree. "These," explained Deva, "are the great men who look after these caves." The men, with obviously little to do save loaf, half-grinned in a sheepish way. But there had been no trace of anything except appreciation and deep humility in Deva's tone.

One of the guides had an electric torch. Trailing the long black wire behind us, we explored the unexpectedly lively recesses of the Jain caves—particularly No. 32.

"The Jains have one high priest," it was later explained to me, "who remains celibate. But the others are encouraged to take the greatest pleasure out of life, so long as nothing is given to harm." The highly practical pleasures of reproduction were especially encouraged; ample evidence of this abounded on the walls and ceilings of Cave No. 32 in the form of fabulously colorful erotic paintings. The delighted expressions, narrow waists and delicious breasts of the dancing-girls took my breath away—and although the pigments had been ground from earth and stone a thousand years ago they still glowed. Age had not dulled the genius of these artists; the work seemed completely fresh. Not just the paintings, which were invisible without the torch, but the sculpture as well seemed imbued with life.

From the Jain caves Deva and I took a long, winding trail which cut above the cliffs and revealed an entirely new set of caves, scattered along the head-waters of the majestic falls. We hopped over a wide ravine where, last year, a tourist had slipped and been thrown to the rocks two hundred feet below. We finally arrived at a stone flank high on the shoulder of mighty Kailasa. The temple loomed almost frightfully within its citadel of basalt. Parrots sailed about within the compound, and striped chipmunks scooted about the sculptures. Vast and solid, Ellora's masterpiece seemed locked in an eloquent, un-approachable silence. When the thunder had passed and the sky showed signs of promise, Deva and I hiked together along the familiar trail leading up Kailasa's south shoulder and up, up, over watery meadows populated by peasants, flies and brilliant orange flowers, to the pools at the falls' headwaters. Our intention was to bathe among the simple upper caves, but as we approached and beheld the ugly brown torrent we began to have doubts.

We hemmed and hawed and poked around in the caves. But the water was filthy. What to do? From the plains below came the thumping of drums—hirelings at Gurukul School, trying to frighten away the birds.

"What would you do, Deva, if I wasn't here?"

"I would bathe."

"Then please, please do!"

A bit more hiking, during which time I was stung by a cactus (this entire trip has been characterized by small, annoying stings), and Deva located an area that was not too turbulent. We stripped—finding to our mutual surprise that we shared a love for bright blue underpants—and hopped from rock to slick rock. Once we arrived, Deva went at it thoroughly, while I simply rinsed arms and legs in the silty current. Couldn't help but admire Deva's wiry, tough physique; he couldn't help but notice my infamous feet, an unending source of peevish embarrassment to me. Still it was a moment of intimacy, shared, like so many things here, in a sphere of unpretentious good humor.

SEPTEMBER 26

On Saturday, September 24, I elected to spend my final day on location visiting the much-celebrated caves at Ajanta. It was not as if I really had the time to spare, it was that I couldn't be so close without visiting them. They're older and much more well-known and touristed than their Ellora buddies, and the emphasis on Ajanta is on the fantastic mural-work hidden within the caves rather than with the sculptures. From my journal:

> We begin with a confessional. Ellora moves me, but Ajanta knocked my socks off. All day I've been running through a sour-grapes routine, trying to convince myself that the Ellora caves are "better." They're certainly more raw, wilder, emptier and more mysterious, but they are not better. The strictly Buddhist Ajanta temples, hewn and painted between the second century BC and AD sixth century are unquestionably state-of-the-art, and I can understand why they are surrounded by gates and curio-stalls and powerlines and fueled by an endless *naga* of tourists.
>
> The paintings are so beautiful. Every element—the scenes, compositions, pigments—achieves individual mastery. Taken together the effect is stunning. With my dear little light-ticket clutched tightly in hand, I went back again and again to marvel at the flying *apsaras*, to

weep at the mural of Buddha taming the crazed elephant Nalagiri, to
feel my heart fill with empathy at the portrait of Sundari discovering
that her husband has decided to renounce the world and become the
Buddha. Every scrap and fragment was a masterpiece. Gorgeous
celestial beings shooting down from the clouds; the superb, sensuous
figures of Padmapani and Vajrapani, bodhisattvas light and dark; the
pink-on-pink dancing girls who, inked from ground lime and
lapis lazuli two thousand years ago, challenge Gauguin and Cezanne
in their luminous grace. Call me stoned, call me spellbound, I was
ready to move into those caves.

Aside from the paintings, several sculptures also thrilled me. Buddhas powerful and robust, virile as all hell and ready to shake the
world...one in particular was surrounded by a border of mythical
crocodiles, horses, and elephants. So profoundly and confidently
etched were the figures that I felt for a moment the panel had to be a
secret door, leading to a vault of untold riches. I kept looking for the
"hidden panel" to open it. For the first time, I could *feel* the sculptor
at work, balanced expertly between improvisation and intent.

SEPTEMBER 27

I don't know; maybe this Indian art is for me what peep shows are for some,
but I can hide under the robe strings of High Art and admire, in the company
of professors and without any trace of perversion, the rounded, jutting pubic
mounds and suppliant asses and luscious, mounded tits of the Hindu apsaras
and goddesses, swelling up inside my own well-worn shorts and occasionally,
this is true, looking about nervously to see if anyone is about and, finding no
one, thrusting myself deeply into the stone...don't tell me those tits don't
come alive, and nudge against me challengingly as I wrestle tongues with
celestial sculpted nymphs and river spirits...don't tell me that fine pubic hairs,
expertly fashioned out of basalt and lava, do not irritate me for hours after
munching the immoveable mounds of Ganga and Jamuna and Saraswati...you
see that professor of Indian Art History, chewing *pan* behind his desk? Read
his book; read between the lines; he's the worst kind of deviant, caught in an
eternal Pygmalion trap. Ellora is filled with gorgeous sculptures of voluptuous
women, and on every one the bodies pulse a dull matte dust gray, but the tits
gleam from constant wear and attention. What can I say? Maybe you want to
hear about What It Was Really Like, and think these are just the ravings of an
ersatz hermit lunatic who's getting closer and closer to believing that everything in this sad, funny world, beginning and ending with women's bodies, is
merely "Maya"—illusion.

Here is a man who has forgotten how to punctuate and has not cooked even spaghetti for months. Here is a man to whom Santa Barbara and *eye* magazine seem like brilliant jewels in the crown of some distant king, lord of a realm where Everything Comes From; a man who, in his oddly solitary and still virtually passion-less existence abroad remembers the awful luxury of those past days the way he once remembered snow-peaked Himals... here is a man who, waxing maudlin, likes to pretend that he would trade it all in if he even had the chance.

38

Today another crazy day. The thin-skinned balloon of my discipline swiftly punctured by the news that, if I do indeed wish to journey up to the Everest region next week, it would be necessary for me to go to the Royal Nepal Airlines building by noon to reserve an air ticket, or else face the weeklong walk in through a nightmarish land of slippery mud and waving leeches. In other words, no choice in the matter. I hopped aboard my scooter and wound downtown through the dust and traffic, only to be confronted by a maze of red tape so thickly and cunningly woven that it took me four and a half hours to procure two seats, which, in the traditional style of the subcontinent, were kept in absolute doubt until the very last possible moment.

The prospect of being out in the Himalayas again—for the first time since 1979—is a tremendous boost to my spirits. Kathmandu has begun to bore me. It's striving all-too-successfully toward the tundra-like millieu of all things twentieth century, and I grow increasingly alarmed at the prospects for this country's future. For some reason every developed country in the world seems to feel it has a stake in this place, a deep and abiding need to drop charity into the great lap of Asia. The result is a sharp rise in available technology, more devices-of-"progress," but without an evolved ecological consciousness to temper them. It's like living in a toy box, but the toys aren't much fun and produce a lot of oily smoke.

*

I have nothing to tell you about art shows, or artists, or social scenes of any kind. Sometimes I play poker Saturday night. I don't drink much. Usually dine out, alone, nodding to the clusters of acquaintances who have stepped out to eat in each others' good company and return home to fuck their respective partners. Don't get me wrong; my famous abrasive cynicism is actually evaporating, if slowly. The interpersonal dramas and back-biting that fueled it at home is absent for me here. I'm like Don Rickles in an isolation tank, hurling pebbles in a vacuum. "But I was a prince," I tell my hallucinations, "in my own land."

"Then go home," the voices advise.

What could be more cruel? Forced into the Best of All Possible Worlds I nibble my nails and jerk off resolutely, combing the corners of my *chakras* for crumbs left by the genius. Frustrated by the knowledge that it's only a missing link, just one little link out of line, but missing is missing, and as I rise to shake the insects out of my shirt, I glance accidentally, always accidentally, at the clock, and marvel at how the time sweeps by unperturbed, when once I thought it was sweeping me toward my destiny.

It's 6 P.M. . . . the kitchen is filled with the acrid stench of an aluminum pot that was left on the burner too long. Someone switches on the radio and tries to find Voice of America, but it's too early. A Dutch friend writes a letter; a fashion designer from Hong Kong packs, picks up and heaves over his shoulder a cache of sweaters that he was photographing in my living room (with an extremely neurotic Italian model). Mildred sticks a knife into the cake she's trying to bake, but it's a lost cause—the person who helped mix up the ingredients confused the milk powder for flour, and the result is a perpetual pudding sloshing around in the oven. A strange evening, indeed, but not atypical. My life in Kathmandu is expanding to fill the shape of its container—me—and, as you know, that's a pretty odd shape.

This letter arrives via "courier." Lots of people coming and going now; it's peak season. Tomorrow morning another friend is returning stateside, and she's mailing this, as well as the photos taken last month while Bill Geary and I were trekking in Gokyo, Chhukung, and Sagarmatha (or, in the vulgate, Everest) valleys.

*

The reason I took the trip was so that I could be in Namche Bazaar—a famous Sherpa trading town near Everest—when my friend Brot Coburn, the UNESCO alternative energy engineer, turned on the electric system he's spent the past two years installing. Hope to write it up for some magazine or other. It was a real gas—I worked with him for about a week beforehand, doing some wiring and generally causing about as much trouble as George Plimpton did for his football team. But finally the evening came, and we all stood on a high rock overlooking the mist-shrouded village waiting for the Swiss engineers in the powerhouse far below to flip the switch at the dot of 6:15. "Keep your eyes on the west side," Brot kept whispering nervously, "for any sign of light. The other half of town isn't wired yet." We stared intently, waiting to see if the lodges housing the switchboxes would short out and catch fire before anything else happened—but then, without even an audible "blink," there was a transformation . . . even from our distant perch, we could hear the children shrieking with delight as the light bulbs suddenly illuminated the entire *east* side of the village. Brot was stunned . . . kept muttering, "Hunh?" but popped the champagne nonetheless. It looked exceedingly strange . . . after 350 years of candle or Coleman light, to see over-bright sixty watt bulbs blazing through the windows. Half expected to see the morgue-blue glow of a television inside some village headman's lodge.

Out in the streets, the kids were singing *"Namchema bijuli balyo!"* Lights are lit in Namche! And Brot walked up through town like a returning war hero, totally ignored by everyone except those whose lights had failed to light. It was a bizarre scene, with champagne and canned quail in the powerhouse, me scribbling inanely in my little notebook, Sherpanis squinting in their lodges, and kids dancing around like they'd just seen God.

For the next three weeks Bill and I explored the three main river valleys of the area. Carried our own packs and managed to survive some freezing weather (to 15-below C) and high altitudes (up to 18,000 feet) without any serious problems. Being at high altitude is weird indeed, and especially unpleasant at night; your lungs forget how to breath, and it's a conscious effort to keep them from falling into an abstract choppy rhythm that leaves you gasping after five minutes. All through the darkened lodges you can hear the labors of lungs making their peculiar and individual adjustments . . . gasping, wheezing, panting, rattling, it sounds like a bunch of Spaulding basketballs getting the air squeezed out of them. But all the problems are more than made up for by the territory. There were some moments when I would come around a corner and literally stagger backward as I beheld the sight in front of me; glacier walls five miles high, waterfalls shooting off the edge of the world, lines of Himalayan peaks so sharp and sculptured that it seemed impossible they'd landed that way by nature's random caprice. From an artistic point of view it was like being sucked upward by a magnet, and face-to-face with those stupendous mountains, I had to feel both arrogant and humbled. Arrogance borne of simply being *animate*, and knowing I had some peculiarity over the scenery, which dumbly and innocently blows your mind; and humility because my mind was blown, and no amount of staring upward with my mouth hanging open could convince the eye/brain team that what it was seeing was as big or as hard or as cold as it was. I began to understand something about why climbers do it; it's fully an ego trip, to be sure, but in the process of fulfilling that power play you really do get to know and to comprehend the mountain in a direct, intimate way that must compare favorably to the anthropomorphised image of fucking its brains out. They're not named after goddesses for nothing.

Along the trail, peering this way and that, I paid much attention to the stones lying about—hoping to find treasure poking from within the crumbling pathside. A fossil, because I know the area was once a great ocean; a gold nugget, to fashion into a pair of simple rings (I won't be ready to marry until magic intervenes); and a very peculiar, unguessable stone to bring home as a gift for the painter Cheryl Bowers. She was mentioning, at my farewell party, the inspiration she'd drawn from a phallic/clitoral stone picked up on a recent venture—surely a certain stone from these staggering ranges, where the Earth's crust buckles and shoots up to form the razor-sharp Himals, would impart its specific gravities to her work. So I searched my secret search, seeking the three rocks of my imagination. Cerebellum stones.

*

Next to the mountains, the most spectacular things were the glaciers, which brought a reverent "Holy shit" from my chapped lips every time I saw one. They're literally rivers of ice, and, like rivers, they flow. If the mountains are a mostly visual thrill, these are aural—the constant sound of the shattering, avalanching ice rings like thunder across the surface of a vast crystalline meringue and you're just a speck upon it. Lots of people die on those things; we could've, too, if we'd stuck around long enough. My favorite sport was to sit on a ridge and watch a glacier for about an hour—pick out one especially huge boulder and wait for it to heave over or something. Watching the glaciers was a reassurance that the Earth is actually alive, and that it'll live on long after the wimpish homo sapiens have pulled a mass lemming over the final edge. Amen.

*

There is a tiny town called Gokyo, two days' walk up the Dudh Kosi (literally, "Milk River") Valley from Namche Bazar. Gokyo was just about unknown three or four years ago; now it's a popular destination for trekking groups.

The town has a magnificent location, which combines all the most dramatic aspects of the Himalayas. Situated beside a sapphire-blue lake, it is separated by a low ridge from the Khumbu's longest glacier. And an afternoon's walk brings you to the base camp of Cho Oyu, one of the world's seven highest mountains. Gokyo itself is nearly 17,000 feet above sea level, which means that oxygen molecules are few and far between—difficult to support a flame.

I told the *didi*—the woman running the lodge—exactly what I planned to do, and she went out of her way to help. I watched as she twisted thin branches to fit between cracks in the stone wall, and set up a little shelf upon them. I picked a flat piece of slate from the edge of a nearby roof and placed it on that precarious shelf, then fished through my pack for the rare prize I'd discovered in Dengboche: a fat, red candle of the slow-burning persuasion.

No yarmulka was at hand, so I used my yak-wool hat. No prayer-book was available, so I simply recited the twenty-third Psalm. It was a piecemeal affair, but I meant well—and grandpa got what I believe was the highest *yizkor* ever.

Interesting reactions from those who knew. An old Tibetan man saw the candle, watched me, then pressed his hands together in a gesture of deep respect (toward the flame); a young Israeli man, member of the crack Entebbe team, expressed his admiration thus: "Even though I myself am not religious, I must say I respect your efforts."

It was a tiny flame, and I had to nurse it carefully, but it did indeed burn the full twenty-four hours—and then some.

*

Arrived back two days ago, and spent the morning drinking self-congratulatory beers and eating spiced peanuts with Bill. By the time I staggered home it was late afternoon, and there was a note on my bed—from Teri. She'd arrived in town, waited a few days, and then set off on a short trek of her own—only hours before! I was blind with frustration; but the note said she'll be back in a week.

Happy New Year. This weekend—these past four days, in fact, have been the holiday of Tijar which is coming to a climax this weekend. It's my favorite festival of the year, and I'm mad as hell Teri opted out on it...had to wander the streets alone last night as bottle-rockets whizzed through the air and manic booms shook the night ("Fuck, where'd they get that dynamite?"). Thursday night was homage to cows; Wednesday was dogs (you mention dogs...you should have heard these mongrels howl as Hindoos chased them down with plates of flowers and red tika-powder...they didn't know they were going to get fed, too); Tuesday was crows. Friday, yesterday, was the local tribal New Year, and it's sort of like that, Christmas and 4th-of-July rolled into one. Tijar means "Festival of Lights," and over the years I guess that's been loosely interpreted to include bombs. My little mustard-oil lamps burned beneath a sky snap, crackle, and popping. You would have loved the scene downtown. A crowd of kids stands in front of a shop, the shopkeeper lights a fuse and tosses the cherry bomb into their midst. At the same instant, all eight or ten kids leap *at* the bomb in a mad race to step out the fuse before it explodes, and win the chance to blow it off themselves. Needless to say they're almost always successful, and you ought to see them crouching with their tongues out over those smoldering one-sixteenth inch long fuses for the relight. They have these firecrackers here that you can hold in your hand as they explode...actually they're the same exact ones we had as kids except that our mothers told us they'd blow our fingers off and their's never did. Now I understand how these Hindoos can swallow cobras without getting nailed; their mother never told them not to.

So there I was in the Kathmandu worth being in, tasting oily bee-swarmed sweets and watching strings of Christmas-tree-like lights blink on and off and on in the lightbulb vendor's stall, innocently holding my sparkler aloft when a huge weird malevolent tide came sweeping down the mobbed alley toward me, and the tide of people parted in panic, leaping back into its own arms as a crazy scared cow came charging at us, horns down and in a big hurry to get out of there...there was screaming and shouting as the maddened animal barrelled through, barely missing a few sets of balls and kidneys as it charged, and then it was past, causing commotion some yards beyond as my section swallowed up the incident without another wink. That happened to me in an Indian train once and, believe me, I know exactly how that animal felt. Like suddenly looking up and you're on a mobbed dance floor on Mars. But between the cow and the firecracker-jumping, I think last night painted a picture of this city in my mind that's bound to remain eternal.

I've pursued the middle-class dream relentlessly here and now I'm suffocating in a gigantic house three sizes too big for me ("because it was there") and wishing I'd gotten a shack and a downtown workspace and played it as it laid instead of trying to tear it all up and start over again. Lack of options regiments your life, whether or not you have an appetite for time . . . and I've nailed myself onto the Volkswagon of my ambitions. You're right that I'm still the little white bird around the big white dream. Some ideas for a book but I'm fighting the walls of some creative shell—it just stretches out smoothly between the life I live and the existence I project for myself.

Outside a cow brays and brays and brays. I used to think they were doing it out of pain or remorse or something, but now I think they simply want to make noise, just like you and me. Well, fuck it; after all, they're sacred, aren't they?


NOVEMBER 12

Another luscious sunset in Kathmandu; I've gotten to the point where I can tune out completely the sounds of the traffic and hear virtually nothing except the little girls playing on the roof next door and the linear squeak of neighborhood birds, which sounds like someone sliding bare-assed down a hot sheet of dry metal. Sitting here in my kitchen surrounded by the abortions of my graphics attempts: scraps of colored rice paper, shards of gods, a tipped-over hash pipe and various stamps of traditional Nepali musical instruments. A cup of finished tea sits by my left hand, the coagulated remains of powdered milk forming doomed associations at its bottom. Everything is lit up in a salmon glow, the sky like lithium at room temperature, the bricks on all the houses outside aging invisibly, purple flowers that never wilt festooning a bronze statue of Tara that also glows, but with a cool eroticism. Teri in the shower. My fate tonight is coughing and typing, trying to catch up on the correspondance that's been giving me dirty looks every time I walk by the "unit" in the living room.

Been trekking through the Solukhumbu (better known as the Everest region) for a while—a good four weeks with a pack on, exploring some of the luminous rivers and staggering peaks that comprise the earth's highest scenery. As far as the Himalayas are concerned, *"no hay dos,"* if you catch my meaning. Only by sitting in the Casablanca in Santa Barbara for seven hours and drinking unlimited Dos Equis while singing Mexican love songs could you begin to appreciate the abandoned drunken ecstasy those mountains produce in a soul; even then, I suppose, it'd be a tough thing to simulate. We were reduced to moments of staggering backward and landing on our asses as we beheld the obvious environmental sculpture of some unknown, untheoretized alien beings who, in my opinion, *had* to have been responsible for carving the

Himalaya; maybe as a Master's project for some university on Alpha Centauri.

The way people carry things. As the Kelty expedition pack wore the skin off my hips, and concentration focused on my throbbing right knee, I watched with wonder and curiosity the porters striding by with miraculous loads slung from straps across their foreheads. Many of them, now, also use shoulder straps, but instead of the hip belt they fortify their support with the cranium. What's the difference? Their hips must be at least as strong as ours; but for some reason they have specially developed a difference in the power of the *chakras*. We carry with the stomach/groin chakra; they with the head. Is the hefting of eighty kilogram loads over Himalayan passes actually an advanced form of meditation?

I brought only one book on the trek: the New Testament. Got through the Gospels and half of Acts before I lost it in Maccherrma, somewhere high above the Gokyo Valley. I liked Acts the best; though Peter had a lot of the elan that Jesus seemed to lack. Still glad to be a Jew. My feeling in general is that Jesus was at his best when he put the miracle aside and worked, like Buddha, from an unshakable sense of justice and balance...like with that woman who was going to be stoned. I always knew he was a headstrong Semetic, but I was surprised at his moments of sarcasm and arrogance; and astounded at the thickness of his disciples! Most frightening, though, is that I no longer see hellfire/ brimstone evangelism as an off-the-wall mutation of "gentle" Christianity...in the light of the New Testament, it almost makes sense. At least, I can see why that kind of preaching has had so little trouble gaining a hold over the masses.

But poor fucking Judas! "It is preordained that I will be betrayed; but woe is the man who betrays! It would be better for that man if he had never been born...." I mean, sounds like a frame-up to me!

A totally different type of faith operates out here. This morning, Teri and I went to see this guy at the National Science Museum. He's been living for the past two weeks in a glass cage with seven dozen snakes. Every kind of snake found in this part of the world, including poisonous ones like krait, cobras and vipers. Twenty-three hours a day (he gets a lunch break) with eighty four slithering reptiles. We talked to him; he's not enclosed totally, but has a sort of large window through which he "greets" the public. His greeting to me was to hand me a couple of snakes. I kind of enjoyed them, although I wasn't ready to stick them into my mouth or down my pants. Needless to say he didn't hand me any poisonous ones...and I could almost see, holding the tactilely interesting and harmless—nay, friendly—snakes, how someone could actually develop the faith and power to live-in with them without getting bit. Daniel in the Lions' Den, right?

Wrong! My attempts to look at the thing in terms of Western theology were shot to hell when the guy informed us that he's been bitten over fifty times, and each time it's agony, and each time he has to be rushed to the hospital to take anti-venom or else he'll "hit the spitoon," as they say. He held out his hands for me to see, and I was amazed at the Mars-like canals of scar and stitching from all the times he'd had to open and suck out the wound.

Well, I'm not sure I remember what my point was in saying all this, except that I was much less impressed with the whole feat once I learned this man wasn't immune to snakes, and a little bit frightened by his motives, which seemed to be little more than a compulsive craving for fame and fortune. That is, anyone could live with snakes and get bit all the time, heh? Face it, this guy was a nut, but he knew what he was doing when he went for the Big Time. Now you see why I've always considered Chris Burden a very "Eastern" artist; fate can indeed be propitiated with sacrifices.

The realization that I've written about so many holy things in this letter makes me a little uneasy. Snakes, the Bible... could this be an example of the so-called "ghost-writing" that people do when they're unconscious, or hypnotized? Alright, you got me... I admit it, I've written this whole thing while asleep, as part of an experiment we're performing at the ashram.

Sneezing and sneezing. *Best of Bowie* on the deck; the sky fading from squashed pomegranate into Nile grape. Teri feels a bit sick, victim of the Kwality-brand ice cream I treated her to around noon. Par for the course. I've had more evenings of borderline barfing than I can recall, thanks to the toothsome *kanna* (food) of Kathmandu. There are prices to be paid for getting out into the world. But before I began to enumerate them once again I will confess that, for all my longing for stateside comforts, I do still love being here, away from the Tupperware Tetracycline Forcefeed, in this land where giant, abandoned, rust-covered ferris wheels can be swarmed by kids who hang and climb and give each other rides without a hint of lawsuit paranoia. Five months into my tenure I peer at the floored balloon of my ambitions, but much enjoy booting it around the room and bending it into neat animal shapes.

*

You really slay me, brother mine, when you complain about how you must nourish your spirit "by exertion of the will alone." Poor guy! What do you think the rest of us are doing? Snorting ahead like some caricature of Mailer or Hemingway, under the rutting madness of hormonal coal? Physically, morally, intellectually and artistically, I and every other writer or artist I know manages to get from breakfast to dinner only be herculean force of will. And nailing ourselves down behind the typewriter or canvas is like trying to convince a five-year-old to eat his poached-eggs-on-toast. Creativity is a slimy, nervous reptile that you're compelled to catch and feed even though the very sight of it fills you with apprehension. Mann was right about that; it is a power, and resisting it is harder than submitting.

Look at yourself! The perpetual student of classics, philosophy, literature! Everything about your lifestyle runs counter to the traditional success ethic we were taught as children. Yet you're irremedially in the grip of your obsessive soul-studies, and well you know I understand your obsession, and never question your motives, 'cause I'm chained to them myself. Fortunately for me, my pound of literary talent is grafted onto a relentless egoism, so I'm continually seeking outlets for my work. One of the world's great ironies is that I can sell this work, so the system feeds upon itself continually. Never has self-worship been more seductive.

Your translation from Mann's *Tonio Kroeger,* slyly introduced as being "on the subject of writing," tickled me:

"He gave himself over to the power that seemed to him the most sublime on Earth, that he felt to be his only calling, and that promised him greatness and honor—to the power of the spirit and of the word, which, smiling, reigns over a dumb and unreflecting world. With his youthful passion he gave himself to her, and she rewarded him with everything she has to give and took from him, implacably, everything she is accustomed to take.

"She sharpened his vision and let him see through the great words that stir the hearts of men; she disclosed to him others' souls and his own; she made him clear-sighted and showed him the inmost recesses of the world and the secret causes that lie behind words and deeds. And what he saw was this: comedy and misery, comedy and misery."

Sadly, those thoughts on the art hardly seem to apply to me... I definitely must agree with Edison's maxim that genius is only 1 percent inspiration and 99 percent perspiration. The first section of Mann's description of writing sounds like the mythical fuck, if you'll allow, while in reality the process has more in common with bringing a woman to orgasm after you've already enjoyed your due. Even when I was writing with youthful zeal and abandon, like the lucky chap in the excerpt, it never seemed to me a dissection of the soul. Maybe I saw the comedy and the misery before the Muse ever undid my belt. Certainly, in retrospect, those two attributes may be said to define both our childhoods.

NOVEMBER 16

Little astounds me anymore about the cultural frappé of Kathmandu. Everybody wears everybody else's fantasies. I understand why they call Lucas and Spielberg the High Priests (read, "Dalai Lamas") of Modern Wizardry... how different is a movie fantasy from a religious one? I guess it all depends whether or not religion is fantasy. How deep you go. If that Sherpa in the *Star Wars* T-shirt can use the Force, who gets the mango? If that porter behind Donkey Kong masters the machine (and remember, these are the matter-masters), perhaps an entirely new infrastructure concerning time and light will reveal itself to him, like the Clear Void the lamas inhale.

Amazing holidays here recently... the local Newari New Year, called "Diwali" (try saying it a few times), was a gorgeous festival of lights and explosions, the kaleidoscopic bazaars packed with people, garlands everywhere, as close as I've come to acid without being on it. Spent a lot of time in the streets, wandering around and petting cows... cows can be beautiful, you know; they worship them here. The squares were filled with bonfires (trash, but who cares? Like love, fire is fascinating no matter what its origins), and the women, beautiful enough to begin with, sort of floated through the madness like visions, in their finest saris...the next day was *Bhai Tika*, or "brother worship," when sisters do this whole ritualistic blessing of their male sibs. My next-door neighbors called me over and treated me to my very own ceremony. A lovely *bahini* (little sister) traced circles on the floor around me with a dampened chrysanthemum, sprinkled my head, shoulders and knees with water from a polished brass spoon, and applied a series of intricate, colorful *tikas* to my forehead before draping a gorgeous lei of fresh flowers around my neck. Felt as native as I've ever felt. One of the brothers took pictures; it was pretty funny because he had no conception of what a focal plane is...held the camera at any given angle, snapping away absurdly at weird tilts and obliques.

NOVEMBER 12

Kathmandu just finished up a run of post-monsoon holidays. A city is a city, but this place knows how to do it up. Perpetual Mardi Gras, beer shooting from the mouths of the idols, water buffalos sacrificed by the score in Ratna Park, glass beads hanging like vines in damp alleyways, illuminated by the glare of naked bulbs; and cows everywhere, staring placidly at the bonfires burning in every little square. The reckless, imaginative and devoted life of the Hindus is just about to my scale, and I draw constant inspiration from the paradoxes and surprises of day-to-day life here.

Today's Thursday, and tomorrow another trek will begin. Teri and I will be up at 5:30 A.M. to board the early bus for Pokhara; from there we'll take a two-week trek north, to the Annapurna Sanctuary.

I'm especially interested in this area because Elena Siff, an artist in Santa Barbara, sent me an article about an environmental sculpture that a New York artist did in that neck of the Himalayas. And I've heard that the Sanctuary itself is God's Very Lap, a bowl of mountains so high and cold and steep that once you're in it's pretty near impossible to see how you entered. But—as on all these treks—the final destination is only a small part of the voyage. Any journey into Nepal's foothills and mountain regions is a trip through the looking glass, and a total escape from the influence of the diesel-breath, dried-apple West; the obscenities of the daily paper, missile deployment and strip-mining, Stallone and slaughterhouses.

I've got to find myself a book to read on the trail. For the Solo Khumbu trek I'd brought along only the New Testament, and ended up wishing I'd also taken a couple of Mickey Spillane novels.

Really, though, it does pay to read the Greats in the wilderness (I use that word loosely here), and I've been searching around for a classic: Conrad or Steinbeck or Salinger, etc. Went into one bookshop and asked the *sowji* for a novel I was sure he must have heard of...he agreed enthusiastically, and searched high and low for a copy. Finally, glowing with satisfaction, he handed me a dog-eared copy of *Kramer vs. Kramer.*

"Yes, yes, this only 'movie book' I have..."

"No, for Christ's sake, not a 'movie book'—I want *Moby Dick!*"

He shook his head sadly, smiling. Well, I suppose it's understandable. If you ask for a copy of the *Ramayana* in Brooklyn you'll probably end up with *Real Men Don't Eat Quiche.*

DECEMBER 8

Bloody cold here in Kathmandu, and life as frantic and ambitious as a pin-ball. Moving out of my overlarge house in a few days (and leaving a furious landlord behind); in exactly one week I'll be in Sri Lanka, to spend a month there on assignment for *Islands* magazine. It's the most important job I've ever had, and thinking about it makes me alternately want to jump through the clouds or piss in my pants.

After that it's back here, back to the mornings and evenings of paralytic cold, the stiff joints and congestion, perpetual chow mein, the wise and stupid menagerie of this mile-high capital.

Returned less than a week ago from the Annapurna Sanctuary, where Teri and I, along with two fellow trekkers named Les and Stephani, cavorted like gnats in an icy bowl, surrounded by 14,000-foot high walls and amazing acoustics. Every little avalanche (there are dozens each day) echoes relentlessly across the sawtooth glaciers, thunderous testimony to powers quite beyond my comprehension.

Thanks to an expert blend of bravado and stupidity, the four of us ended up stranded in the Sanctuary after dark, without tents or a sheltered place to sleep. We'd seen a cave earlier in the afternoon and, hoping to camp in it, had retrieved two of our sleeping bags—but returning to the aerie at sundown we couldn't for the life of us locate the cave. It was an idiom we were almost forced to take literally.

The evening—which happened, we wryly remembered, to be Thanksgiving—was spent huddled around our green wood fire, munching dried fruit, nuts and M&Ms. None of us were especially tired, but by pitch-black 5 P.M., with the temperature plunging, we realized that the only way to live through the night would be to knock ourselves out 'til morning. Don't recall who had the Valiums, but we portioned out 20mg per person and gulped them down. Teri, Stefani and Les crawled into one bag, I into the other.

A fitful night full of that feverish Himalayan moonlight, which has its own way of echoing, just like the sharpest and most terrifying icecracks. . . .

Woke some twelve hours later to purple on the peaks, an iodine stain that spread down Annapurna I and lightened—first to fluorescent amber, then snake-eye yellow. The moment the first rays of actual sunlight fell upon that mountain, an enormous chestplate of ice and snow broke from her highest reaches and roared, skidding and thundering like the Apocalypse, to the glacier below. I leaped from my bag, mouth wide open. The entire Sanctuary filled with a fine, powdery mist, like tooth dust.

Call it whatever you will; I can only see it as some kind of drastic, pure omen of change. Settling on a massive scale; the perpetual free-fall toward equilibrium.

Other adventures on the trail: in the riverside town of Birethanti, a British doctor performed surgery on a squirming porter (pinned down by five of his friends), using my Swiss Army Knife as the scalpel; one frigid night in Ghandruk, a meteor fled across Orion's shoulder as I set the camera up for a time-exposure. Constant reminders that I'm being watched.

Tried something new: spent a day trekking with my Aiwa 'walkman' on, listening to Ludwig van B. and Rachmaninoff as my feet mechanically carried me past waterfalls, down sharp stairways of slate, across raging rivers on popsicle-stick bridges.

Both composers lent an amazing quality of pathos to the trail; especially pronounced was their effect on the waterfalls. Water creates its own rhythm, but is contiguous with almost any other rhythmic template. I was astonished by the way each particular site would be given a totally artificial yet wholly appropriate mood reflecting whatever I happened to be listening to at the time. No place on Earth inspires me more than the Himalayas, and adding the drama of music raised it all to an absurdly poignant level.

Am I living in this world? Sometimes I wonder.

*

"Junk food" looms on the horizon; a blast from the past. Though I dread encountering it, I've heard there's actually a MacDonald's on Sri Lanka. The burgers can't be beef; the island's population is about 30 percent Hindu. Or maybe that's what all the fighting has been about. "The MacDonald's Wars" sparks the conflagration that ignites World War III. Speaking of which, isn't it fun to be out of America? Watching the United States is fun, at least from a healthy distance. Like watching a large and particularly goofy dancing bear trying to slip on a pair of undershorts. Perhaps that exact analogy hadn't occurred to you, but you must admit that Reagan's show looks like a loud and clumsy act.

Catch you soon from the fragrant underbelly.

## SRI LANKA

*Rendezvous with Arthur*

DECEMBER 16

The day's sweltering idiocyncracies—from this morning's dip in the churned Negombo waters to the crazy, billboard-infested ride to nightmarish Colombo —seem like nothing when stacked against the evening's events. An amazingly fine rendezvous with Arthur Clarke on his sixty-sixth birthday, alternately chatting with him (and his housemates) or drinking scotch in his lusciously air-conditioned study, a hammock of exceptionally benevolent technology. An oasis of magic and genius in the equatorial miasma.

The encounter surprised me in many ways, all pleasant. His immediate and unaffected warmth upon seeing me after eleven years; his compulsion to expose me to a vast variety of video segments that were interesting or inspiring or just plain beautiful; his willingness to put himself at ease with me, resulting in what was inarguably the most relaxed and fun time we've ever spent together. He even told me a few characteristically awful jokes, and caught me up on the progress of artists like Kubrick, Spielberg, etc. There weren't a whole lot of slack moments. If his intention was to make me feel at home, he certainly succeeded.

But the crowning touch of the evening was after dinner (his traditional steak-and-kidney pie; I had an omelette and some more scotch), when, against all my protests, he climbed into the back of his sky-blue Mercedes to see me "home." Just driving up those trashed-out streets in that car was an amazing experience...but when we arrived at my mean little lodge he insisted on coming in to meet my friend Les and to sit for a spell in the crowded television-cum-dining room. My Sinhalese hosts regarded him first with suspicion, then with dawning awareness, finally blurting:

"What is your friend's name please?"

"Arthur Clarke."

They were completely flabbergasted to find the first citizen of Sri Lanka standing in their living room, clad in a homely terrycloth robe and grinning like a kid who has just played an enormously successful practical joke. The eldest son—a strapping, stocky professional boxer—ran up to his room to fetch his copy of *Tales of Ten Worlds,* which Clarke jubilantly autographed. It was like The Giraffe Who Came to School, and I was inwardly delighted to have brought the real-live item to "show and tell."

Though Arthur didn't stay long, he left the Sinhalese family with the same impression I'd gathered after a full evening: that of a brilliant, modest man, enormously interested in people and generous with his very crowded time.

My second visit to Arthur's, like the first, was characterized by an infusion of video images. Among the video segments he screened for our benefit: scenes from *Raise the Titanic*, a documentary about how to photograph sharks, the opening sequence from *Blade Runner*, a Jean-Michel Jarre concert filmed live in China, the opening of *Day of the Dolphin*, the dog scene from *The Thing*, an interview with Frank Oz, a scene from a cult-flick called *Artemis 81*, Stanley Kubrick's daughter's film of the filming of *The Shining*, and a special about the divers who discovered the Edinburgh's five tons of gold beneath eight hundred feet of ocean.

Arthur cooked a cheesy Welsh rarebit for lunch—according to his housemate Valerie, this was the first meal he's cooked in Ceylon for years. Dessert was the fruit salad we'd brought, and ice cream, which Arthur provided.

After the second visit to "Leslie's House" I still wonder about the man. Brilliant, busy, a total video-addict capable of staring at the screen for hours; a prankster, young at heart, living a strange and isolated second childhood; a man, to be sure, of many mysterious worlds.

Toward four we went to the Otter Club together. He on an absurd little stingray bicycle, I on foot. I felt extremely affectionate toward the man as I wheeled him along by the bike's "sissy-bar". We joked our way down the street, object of many bemused stares. Unfortunately, the Otter was closed on account of full moon *puya* day—no ping pong.

Gamini, our proprietor's son, took us along a series of narrow back roads toward a Buddhist temple; one that, he claimed, had a lovely situation. He gave us the fascinating news that the sixty-nine-year-old head monk had died just two days ago, and would be lying in state until the twenty-eighth, at which time he would be cremated and his ashes tucked snugly into the monastery's *dagoba*.

When we arrived at the base of the long stairway to the temple it began to rain like hell; huge drops thwacking off rows of yellow plastic prayer-flags, running in rivers from the gutters formed by palm-leaves above us. We ducked into the nearest house.

"There is no problem," Gamini assured us. "This is my uncle's sister's house." Everyone on this island seems to be related....

Gamini gave the rain ten minutes. We sat in the blue-walled living room as a woman stitched polyurethane prayer flags. A bunch of kids watched our every move. Strange portraits of pretty brides smiled wanly from their frames, tinted with ghostly hues. A small television sat dormant behind a lace cloth. The family asked me how Nepal compares to Sri Lanka. I had to confess there was very little comparison to make. Ceylon is infinitely more developed, with the fruits of technology accessible to even the middle classes. The free-market philosophy shows in every home. I can't help but wonder if Nepal will be forced to make some changes after the upcoming introduction of television; it certainly changed Sri Lanka when it was inaugurated eight years ago.

The rain eased up, and we climbed the stone steps in a clearing drizzle. The saffron robes of the monks we passed delighted me; such a buoyant, human color. There was the inevitable cadre of youngsters—"monk-ies"—as curious about us as we were about them.

We reached the main hall: an open pavilion, long and wide, within which the dead abbot lay. He had been placed upon a dais which rose from the middle of the structure, cordoned off by ropes. A tiny oil lamp flickered by his head. He looked unbelievably small, wrapped in a saffron-orange bag with only his head protruding . . . small, still and absolutely pacific. So compelling and sympathetic was his final repose that I could scarcely believe his life had ended—it seemed that by the slightest touch (psychic or otherwise) he could be persuaded to open his eyes, sit up, and get on with an energetic life. Perhaps, on another plane, that's exactly what was happening.

The dead monk had a profound effect on me, and argued eloquently the beauties of Buddhism. Never could I imagine death presented in a less frightening manner, or with more grace.

Gamini had mentioned that I ought to feel free to photograph the deceased, but surrounded by that spiritual presence I felt sure it would be offensive. I could not have said for certain that the monk himself wouldn't mind. Gamini again assured me: "It is quite alright! The man is a relation of mine!" Indeed, when I set up the photo I was forced to readjust as the living monks crowded into the frame. Finally I got a few good snaps: the tranquil abbot, framed by huge elephant tusks (an unlikely tribute to a Buddhist, I thought!), offset from a background of lush greenery, silver with rain.

JANUARY 7

Sigiriya by bus and auto-stop, after a quick lunch. We drove through some heavy rain, but by the time we were approaching the sky-fortress the weather looked more optimistic.

The sight of that immense butte, thrusting out of the lowlands like an enormous thumb, is stunning. It immediately reminded me of Devil's Tower, or the desolate monoliths of Monument Valley. We checked into the Government Rest House and started off at once toward the fortress—hoping to catch, as Clarke recommended, the late afternoon light on the frescoes. I had guessed their situation from his *Fountains of Paradise,* and our arrival at the site erased any doubts. They do indeed reside in an impossibly precarious niche, cut into the outcropping's massive western wall.

The Lord's been with us today—Lord of Light. It was a long climb, but at its end we found the most precious commodity of the season: low, buttery sunlight filled the gallery, and the luscious maidens of Kasyapa's harem came to life. High above the meticulous Pleasure Gardens, on a steel walkway clinging vertiginously to the cliffside, I spent an hour admiring those ancient beauties and letting their immortal charms pulse in my groin. Slender, muscular and lavacious, they regarded each other with the same cool affection they've known for centuries. Like the endless ranks of admirers who have risen and returned to dust over the past fifteen hundred years, I tried not to take their legendary aloofness personally.

It was a moment of pure magic, among those maidens—the twenty who have survived countless rains, lashing winds, and even vandals. "Poetry," I wrote in the guest ledger. "May they live forever."

JANUARY 8

Sigiriya: a name like a chisel striking stone. We patrolled the fortress early, just as the sun pushed its yolk over the horizon. A blue mist hung around the summit, then cleared. Our guide was already waiting for us.

What a fantastic, terrifying place! The paranoia, arrogance and genius of Kasyapa combined in just the proportions necessary to immortalize him. And, no matter how much history and the *Chronicles* have defamed the man—or how earnestly monks and the elements have worked at defacing his architecture—I could only catch a breath of admiration. To have an insane dream is one thing; to carry it out quite another. Such actions almost never escape human notice. Witness Ellora; the pyramids; Napoleon; the Apollo program. And tangential to my infatuation with Sigiriya is my admiration for Clarke, whose *Fountains of Paradise* drew fascinating parallels.

Our guide led us through the low labyrinths, discoursing on the Cobra Hood Cave, the baths, and the niches we'd seen far up the cliffside. Sentries were posted there, and in order to keep from falling they had to cling to the stones; an excellent tack for keeping them alert. Though much has been made of the entrance—a huge, gaping lion's maw, of which only the enormous claws remain—I was less impressed with the architecture than with the concept of the entrance as a whole. What an effect it must have had on visitors, to traverse that final hundred yards! As our guide insinuated, it was not necessarily the lion *itself* that struck awe and terror into their hearts, but the realization that they were about to meet a lord powerful enough to have his way even with stone.

From the claws to the windswept aerie the path cuts steeply up the face of the rock, and one must cling, for dear life, to the railing. To slip would be fatal. All along the route are wasps' nests—currently abandoned, thank God. Those transient wasps are more than a nuisance; legend holds that they are the bitter reincarnation of Kasyapa's slaves. They punctuate their periods of residency by swarming, attacking everyone in sight, to the point where a screened cage has been built on Sigiriya's summit. This is not to contain the wasps; it's for the tourists. But the cage is outdated, and small. When the furious wasps made their last surprise raid from the jungles on New Year's Day 1984, every single visitor was stung.

We climbed ever so cautiously to the top....

To stand on Sigiriya in the early morning, as sunbeams pierce the clouds and search the landscape below, is an experience that defies allegory. It's easy to see how, installing himself in such a fortress, a man might truly convince him-self—and everybody else—of his immortality. And who knows? After all, no outside enemy slew Kasyapa, and perhaps he would have lived forever if his brother's advancing armies had not moved him to drive a dagger into his own throat.


                                                            JANUARY 15
Gibbous/ this day our daily bread. Out at sea, catamarans like devil-eyes on the horizon. Clear winks of orange. The ocean bright beneath a waxing moon, criss-crossed with powerful waves. Arrack; cigarettes; a little night music. While Teri heads over to Sri Gemenu's to settle last night's bill, I ponder again the possible directions my article can take. Thrown into the pushy blend of guilt and inspiration that evolves from reading good short stories. Like a boy late for school, I anticipate the chide of passing hours. Beggary within and without. But it's much easier to tolerate the pleading of my geared-up muse than abide Sri Lanka's ceaseless "you give me."

A bike ride down the coast from Unawatuna, looking for photos and what-ever else. A quiet Sunday, if not for the buses. Impossible to be left alone; I was followed everywhere by the inevitable rudeness, everyone with a hand out for something. It is somehow intolerable for me to see healthy, well-dressed children begging. What can I say? I must be getting tired of this country. At least, of the people.

But the sunsets at Unawatuna never grow old. During the late afternoon Teri and I strolled slowly along the beach, dragging our feet through the fine sand, powdered mica and pulverized seashells. As the light fell we walked a few hundred yards south and watched the sky throw feathers of red and white around the moon. There couldn't be a prettier place—utterly sedentary and timeless, a sharp contrast to the static roar of the Himalayas.

Even a mere forty-eight hours on the beach leaves me restless. I look forward to the frenetic finale of the next few days—masks, snorkeling, a last encounter with Clarke, and a hopefully successful voyage (I dare not call it a pilgrimage) up the much fantasized steps of Sri Pada: Adam's Peak. Altogether I have a feeling that Sri Lanka will be more of an enigma to me when I leave than it was before I arrived.

My cigarette, tossed to the beach, describes the comet-like death of a firefly. No phosphorescence in the sea tonight, but a kind of sad glow within me.

JANUARY 20

It was like a dream after all, although I'd hoped for a more fantastic morning ...the endless upward climb, begun at 2 A.M., reminiscent of Dahl's *Escalator,* through a darkness punctuated by drink-stalls and the distant glimmer of incandescent lights burning like moonstones all along the twisting route to Sri Pada's mysterious peak. We climbed and climbed, watching the sky hopefully as the moon flitted between clouds. Would it clear? Would the dawn sun break cleanly over the horizon, casting Sri Pada's famous shadow—a perfect blue pyramid—onto the landscape below? There was never a moment when we knew for sure.

Sometimes the stars seemed ready to burst out above us; then there were the hours shrouded in mist. Mist, hashish, the cold, wet railing and eternal hope— somnambulant, we clung to ourselves within these forces as the steep steps loomed forever in front of and above us.

We took frequent breaks at tea-stalls, especially once we felt we were nearing the summit. After the last of these (320 steps below) we emerged to find the moon gone, and clouds layering the sky. This, finally, was a grim and definite indication that our long-anticipated journey would not see the climax we had longed for. From that point until the dawn itself it would be hope-beyond-hope, a perpetual self-calming rosary of doomed "maybes."

Up on top, the shrine awaited us with utter impassivity. Everything tidy, freshly painted and ready to receive the expected generations of devotees. Needless to say I wasted little time in locating the Footprint of Buddha (or Adam or Shiva, take your pick) that gives the mount its name. I was hardly surprised to find it completely ambiguous, a meter-long depression ringed by a cement wall. The concavity could have been caused by anything—except, of course, a human foot. I can barely convey my wonder at the leap of faith—and imagination—required to decide that the rough, oblong depression atop Sri Pada had had anything to do with a man's foot. Still, the pilgrims come in droves—and, bowing, they touch their heads to the stone and pay homage.

I lit a candle and a few sticks of incense and rang the bell three times, perhaps too loudly. The bell is rung to indicate a pilgrimage *completed,* and so the present one is not supposed to be counted. I suppose I was celebrating the

Sri Lanka voyage as a whole—my success in just getting there, for one thing. Ironically I now feel I must go back, to see that elusive shadow which I still, sadly, cannot believe we missed.

The sky lightened, but the rising sun was lost in a band of low-lying clouds. The metallic chanting of resident monks rang out over a primitive loud-speaker, encouraging the dawn. Shapes of hills and lakes began to form on the landscape below—a fabulous place filled with wraith-like clouds. Soon drums were heard, and a little *puya* procession circled the truncated summit, but the spirited little parade only increased my disappointment. And then there was a single, awful moment, somewhere around 6:30 A.M., where a reflected glow hit redly around the eastern rim of hills, and we giddily believed we might have miscalculated, and this was the true, brilliant dawn... but it was only an illusion. I couldn't help but feel a little bitter. Throughout this entire trip, the weather has conspired to flatten our highest hopes for spectacular visuals.

Near seven we decided to descend—or, if you will, surrender. We hadn't taken ten steps when the sun suddenly broke blindingly above its fortress of clouds. I leaped back up the steps, astonished and desperate, hoping beyond reason to see the shadow which, I knew in my rational mind, would have vanished many minutes ago. Les, Stephani, and Teri continued downward.

I was indeed too late to see the pyramid—that effect was long gone. But the morning mists enveloping the peak did not let me leave empty-handed. Even if the specific sight I'd waited a month to see failed our rendezvous, I was able to witness another, even more rare phenomenon. This was an illusion called the "Specter of the Brocken." Seen from the shrine's vertiginous edge, my *own* distended shadow seemed to shoot out into the mists, ringed by a brilliant nimbus of rainbow hues.

Perhaps there's a moral there somewhere; I don't know. But the main non-event, and its stunningly ego-centric finale could easily provide the foundation for a short story.

The walk down was steep and quick, but Adam's Peak was piquish to the last—hiding uncooperatively behind clouds and depriving me of the photos that were my due. Finally, for a few seconds at least, it emerged from the mists for a reluctant portrait. I snapped away. But I must confess that I dread the inevitable: climbing that monstrous stairway again someday.

Among the more concrete symbolic transitions in a writer's life is the changing of the typewriter ribbon. This communication is the first thing written on the only spare ribbon I brought to Asia. It's fair to say that, with the loading of this innocent black ribbon, my time in Asia takes on finite dimensions. Eight months is not an unrespectable length of time, and I feel more and more that either (a) something gives birth soon or (b) I should consider changing the names of the streets I'm wandering down late at night.

Sri Lanka, in retrospect, was maybe a little bit more of a vacation than it ought to have been. I'm left now with at least twenty-five pages of notes (spent the past three days putting them in order) and a biggish question in my head: how to tie it all together? Somehow, in four thousand words, I've got to say something brilliant, cohesive and above all original about one of the most elusive countries in the world. I needn't tell you that I've spent a large portion of the time since my return wrestling down panic, an irresistable contention that I've finally managed to bite off more than I can chew. You and I both know that's bullshit—my big mouth can accomodate an elephant whole—but until the actual writing has taken shape I won't believe it's forthcoming.

That's one thing about myself I hope will someday change. The stories get written with or without the anxiety, *eye* comes out with or without the anxiety, life moves on and death approaches with or without anxiety, and if the East has a lesson to teach it is that the anxiety is simply unnecessary. If I learn that one thing out here, it will be enough.

GROUNDHOG DAY, 1984

Oof—it just hit me: an image of old Santa Barbara so clear that my brain could taste it. Do you guys ever think about me when you're walking up Ortega Street? Anyhow that was the image I just got, you sort of in a half-slump between something that happened in one place and something that happened in another. Stopping for fries at Ernie's, don't you know.

For two or three months now I've been on this kick that something closely resembling a hinge is approaching in my life. I still feel that way and I still don't know why. Like there's an opportunity for me to bust out of my laziness, get something done, etc., etc., etc. Well the first base was, as I knew, the story for *Islands,* the Sri Lanka story that had to meet two personal qualifications: it had to be oriented toward a fairly upper-rung audience, and it had to say a couple of original things about Asia in general and Sri Lanka in particular.

Well old chap I think I did it, and even as I sit here basking in the Wyeth sunlight of Groundhog Day the manuscript is at the typist's, slinking along the

face of a cathode ray tube and straightening its tie. It has the twin qualities of
bullioncy and terskiness, which is to say it's incontestably the longest and best
story I've written this year—rising easily above its lack-of-competition, since it
is also the only story I've written this year.

Unlike a lot of people I spend time with out here—including Teri—I do not
feel in the least as if the benefits of the "real" world, career opportunities and
so on, are passing me by out here. I don't feel there's some tight golden spring
in America that's winding up for the stroke of gold in the Land of Gold, and
I'm sure not racing anyone to the mines. Barring a complete reversal of
luck—and believe me, it wouldn't take much to pop the current balloon—I
could probably stay here indefinitely and write all kinds of things. Let me
assure you, I know how Ed White must have felt when he "playfully" refused
to climb back into the capsule after his Gemini spacewalk. How often do you
find yourself in orbit?

FEBRUARY 3

I really like it in this hotel. Sitting on the balcony in the sun as Roxy Music applies
electroshock to my brain and my sunglasses filter out all but the most essential
information. Before I sought perfection: the fancy house, the formica table, the
tiled tub, whereas this time I sought only the sun, a desk that fit into it, and an
electrical socket.

It's a room of my own, but Teri, who stayed on a while in Sri Lanka, could
show up anytime. You know how we feel about the women. I miss the gal, sure
enough, but which way for me after she gets here? Do I still get these 9:30 A.M.
- 4:30 P.M. days in the sun, with only the typewriter and the hash pipe as my
buddies? Do I still get to toss myself around the room at night, drinking
whisky and chewing mildew off the walls? Will I be able to sit up late reading
*Carry On, Jeeves* or will life become one prolonged erection? Like I always said,
Nepal is a country of paradoxes.

Feel like I'm in a little boat somewhere. The air is always filled with the high
hiss of water pumps. Listening to that part on *Avalon* that sounds like an ogre
chewing his spinach. Waiting for the next jet to pass overhead. Motor-
chainsaws grinding along the street. They'll black the power out soon.

Had an amazing experience the other night. It was only my second night
back from Sri Lanka and I wasn't used to the cold, so I went downstairs and
grabbed a heater from the coolies' room. Get it? Anyway, the thing wasn't in
working order, I guess, so I screwed around with it a bit and got it to the point
where everything seemed to be more or less together. By that time it was, say,
9 P.M., and pretty cold. My breath was steaming in the room. So I plug the
thing in and nothing seems to be happening, just a little sparking and sizzling
from around the contacts.

Suddenly there was a terrific explosion, and the whole neighborhood lit up like a torch. All along the street the powerboxes were shorting out, and wasps of blue electricity ripped across the lines, cracking like whips. It was like a movie of Iwo Jima being projected on all the buildings. Better than Tijar...you would've loved it. Tried it again the next night, after they'd worked all day on the lines, but no dice.

FEBRUARY 5

There's a terrific new restaurant in Thamel called the San Francisco Pizza House, and, as is true of more and more of Nepal, it's possible to walk into the place and fairly forget that you aren't upstairs at the Front Room or something. Quite unnerving, to see those posters of cable cars on the wall, those snappy technicolor placemats of the Golden Gate Bridge, Lombard Street, you name it. Writing those names I feel an attack of that surrealistic displacement—knowing you're actually there, I'm actually here, feeling no separation although I acknowledge the contradiction. I seem to have become capable of changing homes like a hermit crab, but any slight stimulus is capable of launching me into fits of nostalgia.

An astonishing event is going on right now, quietly, but in a way that will last forever. A fifteen-minute walk from Bodha, there's a muddy little rice field, a gross little place with nothing to recommend it at all. About a month ago, three little water-spouts formed in the ground, bubbling up from an unknown underground source, and the paddy, still muddy and disgusting, became a fetid little pool. Then the clincher: a farmer working nearby saw two snakes, *nagas*, rise slowly out of the water, look around, twine their necks together, then descend back into the depths. He hauled over a friend, who saw it too. A recurring phenomenon....

Well, it's amazing to watch what's going on around that little swamp. Exactly the process that would occur if the image of Jesus appeared on a tree or something. People are setting up refreshment stands, taking up collections to build a shrine, reporters are arriving to photograph the serpents, the place has become festooned with prayer-flags and there's even an electric light hung just over the place where the nags emerge. I visited the spot myself last weekend; waited like a fool with a mob of people, squinting in the sun and staring at the murky surface. Well, it wasn't all in vain—up came one of the nags—(there may be as many as nine, all different colors), as weird and inscrutable as if it were made of plastic. It peered out of the water like a periscope for about ten minutes, then pulled slowly under again. No sooner had the creature disappeared than the theories and speculations began to fly. "Just wait," said one man, "and you'll see five more: all of different colors!" Another guy, a Tibetan, insisted the snake *was* plastic. But an old woman quickly reprimanded him, reminding the guy that the last person to disparage the herp was killed in a car accident the following day ... and so on. But it's rather a miraculous thing to watch, a rare process. For eternity, perhaps, this muddy little pool will be remembered as a holy spot. And I must admit, that was a pretty weird-looking snake.

What's happening? The sound of hammers, and rain-sharpened razorlight, the drying clothes I squatted over all morning wet again, the damned inscrutable cows still out there somewhere, gunmetal clouds but no rainbows. And here I am in the middle of it all, feeling a little sick from too much coffee and too many Yak cigarettes and whatever duty-free Real scotch gets wiggled in. Sitting in a hotel room full of the paraphernalia of a scatterbrained existence. You name it: tea-bags from Ceylon, thumbtacks from China, Hero Ink, cassettes spilling their guts onto the gutted carpet, and issues of magazines scattered over the chairs. The Souvenirs of a Solitary Tourist, no doubt. What's it all for? Moving my gravitational center ten thousand miles away has not loosened my private, peculiar grip.

This is the land where the State is religion, the culture is religion, the art is religion, and religion is performance. From the daily decapitations at Dakshin-kali to the steaming altars heaped with flowers, there's always a drum beating at you from someplace. I and those like me live like tweezers, pressing together the polar sides of our western/eastern perceptions to pick out the sharp points. I don't know if it's a blessing or a curse, but it gets easier and easier to just be yourself, wherever you happen to be. This isn't D.H. Lawrence's Asia, engulfing you like the slippery thighs of the medicine-man's wife; closer maybe to Pygmalion, although you never know when the stone is going to burst into life.

Stopped my bicycle on the glaring, dusty road today and watched a cow watching a crowd watching a mechanical crane. The crane operator is bummed because the lever's jammed. The crowd is bummed because the show is stalled. The cow is bummed because yesterday's field has become tomorrow's slum. I watch impassively, but the taxi driver behind me is bummed, and blasts a good one at me—one like you'd never hear in the States. And so ends my reflection on the spiritual: with the realization that once cows are no longer holy here, the whole system will start leaking as fast as a spastic udder. It's leaking already, of course; that, I suppose, is why I'm here. Not to patch the leaks, of course, but to lap up the goods. Any decaying culture passes through a period of great sighing, and those sighs deserve to be recorded.

Life in Asia in general has been active, dissettling, enlightening. My journeys into the mountains were full of visual delights, sculptural inspirations, and literary ideas which will someday find their way into print. Still wrestling with the barbed wire around my own preconception of what a novel ought to be...it's as if I'm waiting for a specific original form to reveal itself. Attempts to slap a plot together around the expatriate community prove superficial; my mind often leans toward science-fiction. I guess that's because the most typical question one asks oneself here is, "What will this place be like after another twenty or fifty years?" One can't help but see the dense inner heart of Buddhism dissolving like a Fizzee in the stew of egg-slicers, 100 percent nylon socks and traffic jams. It seems to me that when a religion or culture finally gets broken, it's because something has cut the cord connecting a people and their raw materials. In other words, you really can predict the downfall of a nation by the fabric of its socks. So in my drugged, inspired moments I engineer a vision of Kathmandu in the year 2010 (2000 seems too close) and plug in Yoki Fang, my miracle-cleaner character.

At the present time Yoki is writing letters to the editor of the *Rising Nepal* (or the *Rising Nepali*, as we like to call it), the country's only legitimate daily (this is fact, not fiction). I've adopted the pseudonym not so much to hide myself as to help me develop this guy through the letters he sends (I'll send you some copies when they're in print)...that is, I'm trying to write these letters from the point of view of someone who lives here thirty-odd years in the *future*. It's an interesting experiment, since quite a bit of my best writing finds its way into letters.

Morning now, after another semi-nightmarish night behind earplugs as the neighborhood dogs plowed through an endless orgy of yelping. There's one dog in particular, just behind my hotel, that I'm seriously thinking of killing. But the question is how to do it. Poison? Beat it to death? Maybe I ought to just head over with a sack and take it away to a dump somewhere. You think I'm delirious, eh? Not so...and certainly not Buddhist enough to go without sleep a third night.

FEBRUARY 8

I look around my room, and what do I see? Tiger Balm, a roll of pink toilet paper, various found objects in assorted states of decay. Reticence to give up secrets. I can't help but wonder where I'd be if I were actually serious about it all.

I can still listen to Rachmaninoff. Sometimes I wonder if that's all that counts. Very difficult to live with so much going on in one's head; I mean, take the scatterbrained bullshit that typified my life in America and cloud even that with another layer, a thick, gooey lacquer called Asia. Walking down the dust-filled street I ponder the future of my writing, wonder why I can't get through (or into) Lessing, and suddenly all is interrupted as I spy a little abstract metal shape twisted on the ground, like some map of Sri Lanka by Walt Disney, and just as I lean forward to pick it up a cow starts pissing on it, and I back away into a begger who scampers off on his twisted foot-stumps, like a crab, recovering my balance just in time to see a black-haired French woman pass by with a copy of *Newsweek*, Ronald Reagan's face sinking on the cover. Cheers. And thank God for Rachmaninoff.

All hail Rachmaninoff. What more romantic figure? One of Russia's youngest and most prodigious pianists and conductors... "Why don't you compose?" So he does, and his first symphony is a flop. Really gets scathing reviews, the kind no one even dares give any more. The man has a nervous breakdown, spends the next four years under hypno-therapy (this in the 1800s) and finally writes Piano Concerto no. 2, which I'm listening to now. It's compositional hypnosis; like Tanguy and Rousseau and Rodin peering out of a Mondrian. You can't escape the eyes.

I'm feeling disturbed, now that the Concerto has come to its inevitable conclusion, and even the applause has died. Like an infant who's lost his rattle, I can think of nothing but blind rhythm. Walk on air... even the clouded dusk sky is baby-blue. Can't help but think of dinner. What'll it be tonight? I live in a hotel room at the moment, so I never eat at "home." Kathmandu offers a whopping variety of restaurants, though... which goes to show that even the most exotic can become contemptible with over-familiarity. Shall it be Indian food, in that shiny little bistro that smells like piss? Or shishkebab and borscht in the Red Square, where the waiter's an obnoxiously over-accommodating Paul Simon look-alike? How's about the Norling, where I found a wire in my ravioli and a grasshopper in my chow mein? Aw, why not the Cimbali? Who cares if they never clean the tablecloths? And buffalo-meat lasagne's *pretty* close to the real thing... do you see my dilemma?

Time to face it like a man.

FEBRUARY 12

Listening to Ella Fitzgerald. Teri, back from Sri Lanka, is singing along.

Much thinking about future plans, the possibilities and opportunites afoot. I still feel a crazy kind of loyalty to my original plan which was, of course, to write a novel out here. My already spawning guilt blossomed into panic when I had lunch with Andy, a kid from the University of Wisconsin College Year Abroad program who also came out here to write his Great Asian Novel. The only difference between his novel and mine is that his is written and mine isn't.

Andy's work casts my situation in sharp relief, and the result is that I've been plunged into a maelstrom of self-searching which has included such queries as, "can I force myself to write a novel?" and, "what if I'm not interested in forcing myself to?"

Strangely enough, the end result of all this has been to open up an acceptance, to silence my internal critic enough so that the ideas can flow in. The past few days have seen a loosening that might lead to anything. You see, the one item that's been so elusive for me is something that Andy brought with him to begin with: a theme, an keystone without those barely connected snatches of brilliance tumble into rubble. Now maybe I've got one—and all that remains is for me to convince myself that writing the novel can spring from curiosity, not ambition.

This is a tense period for me. I feel a strong, accurate sense of suspension. Brazilian music replaces Ella on the Sanyo. I wish I was leading the kind of life that would be filmed with a soundtrack of Latin music; as it is, they'd probably use Burl Ives.

FEBRUARY 13

Writing to you on the edge of a moment, from the aristocracy of limbo. As everything in my life stands poised at the threshold, I wait on the needle and weight it all. It's the time; hard to forget there are twenty-two days until my thirtieth birthday. Such a convenient symbol, that number! Everybody loves to look through that **O**. As I peer in, I see years of youth ahead, nothing to force me into a leitmotif, the world cracking open like a confetti-filled egg, that great, great thing I've got to do still a mystery. It's like hitch-hiking; never think you'll make it, but the ride always comes. As the highway rushes by, those agonized hours of doubting just blow off.

I'm just a few steps beyond the average man. We all wrestle with hope and with luck. They pin us down and drool on us.

VALENTINE'S DAY

Today is *Bhimsen Puja*—one of the less festive holidays, at least in my book. Teri and I rode down to the Bhimsen temple this morning in the hope of seeing the celebration. Just a lot of people lined up in front of the stairs, holding brass trays full of ritual ingredients and bound-up roosters. Ah, the perils of being a male...I told Teri just this morning that there might be a cock sacrifice.

The upper floor of the temple was crowded, smoke pouring through the wooden windows, flames jumping visibly within. Not much shrieking from the roosters; indeed, they were carried passively toward their fates, heads bowed, and emerged down the rear stairway kicking, but headless. That's what I call futility! The people came down holding the decapitated fowl, sometimes by the legs, sometimes in pink plastic shopping bags.

"Hi, honey! Did you get the chicken?"

Some of the women had a gleeful, faraway look in their eyes; still hot from the passion of the sacrifice. One or two looked postively predatory. It gave a strange, erotic lilt to their features.

It's been a week since I've typed anything, so please forgive me if this turns out a little sloopily!

On February 18, Teri and I set off for the Chitwan National Park on Nepal southcentral border. We departed at dawn, a long bus ride out through the hills, down south to the Terai—Nepal's flat, dry plains that become continually hotter and less pleasant until they finally become India. From the bus terminal in Tadibazar we took an oxcart the remaining half-dozen kilometers, arriving at the sachet of lodges and little shops in Sauraha, surrounded by the jungle.

Unlike the mountains, Chitwan Park isn't livid with tourists. Many of the lodges are extremely expensive; like Tiger Tops, which borders the other side of the park and costs upwards of $150 per night. For some reason the cheaper accomodations on the northeast don't get very much publicity, and not many people bother to make a first-hand investigation. Teri and I discovered a very fine group of hut-type lodges that cost us twenty rupees—about $1.20—a night, and used those as a base for a number of fascinating forays into the jungle, on foot and on elephant-back. An amazing variety of game—we spotted monkeys, wild boar, an infinite number of peacocks, and crept cautiously along the path as rhinos prowled within eyeshot.

*

All night long, thunder rolled across the Terai; long barrels of sound following brief flashes of light. Rain came too, whacking against the grass roof of our hut. My feet sweated inside the heavy down bag. It was hard to sleep. Far off, somewhere across the plains, a wedding was in progress, and a loudspeaker blared at top volume. The sound carried over an incredible distance, mutating obscenely along its way. Sometimes it was an eerie keening wail, like demons shrieking in the night. Sometimes it arrived as loud, distorted voices, or a low beat. They turned it off when the rain became heavy, and put it back on as soon as the rain stopped—it went on and off all night.

Ray Rodney knocked on our door at 5:30 A.M. to get us up for the elephants, but it was raining and thundering and we all stayed in bed. An hour later, though, he woke us up again, and this time I could hear that Mike and Nancy were up, too...Mike called that the sky was starting to clear, so we hurried into our clothes and started off for the elephant encampment.

It was a very beautiful morning. The moon was up, low and gibbous in the west, and the Manaslu Himal was slightly visible above the haze. The rain had dampened down the trails, and though they were a little muddy it was better than dust. A fine mist hung over the ground. There were goats and chickens running around, pumps squeaking, and naked children staring at us as we passed by. Nobody asked us for money. We made good time, afraid of missing the elephants, but stopped briefly now and then to spot birds—Ray especially. I remember seeing three or four peacocks up in a frugally flowering tree.

The elephants were waiting for us, standing on the dewy ground with *malis* on each of their backs. We climbed the mounting platform—Teri and I got on the first, largest elephant, whose name was Laxmi Kali. Nancy and Mike boarded the second, Ray got aboard the third, which was very small in comparison to the others. The elephants all had cushions on their backs, and ropes for holding on. We sat with our legs 'way apart, one on each side of the elephant, and hung onto the ropes as we climbed a rise and descended into the river, crossing into Chitwan.

It was great to be in the jungle, riding those elephants—a very safe feeling. The air was full of bird-cries, and whenever the sun broke through the clouds the green of the leaves and blackish-green grasses glowed with electric luminescence. We saw spotted deer, samba deer, and a lot of rhinos. The elephants surrounded the rhinos in the brush and scattered them. Strange animals! The horns, made of compressed hair, like a stubby gouge; those tiny, stupid eyes; the folds of armor across their shoulders and plating their butts; the too-small ears, like jade plant leaves, wiggling in every direction atop log-like heads. Not friendly, these creatures; they looked like throwbacks to the age of dinosaurs. We followed one male for quite a while—he stopped every few yards and pissed like a firehose.

When we returned into the jungle, our *mali* separated from the other two and made his way up an oblique trail. We were confused, but not displeased. The fewer people the better, as far as spotting game is concerned. We wandered into the trees and saw some deer, then stopped dead.

Teri saw the leopard first. It was up in a tree ahead of us, a freshly killed deer in its jaws. The whole thing lasted only a few seconds—the leopard saw us, grabbed its prize and scuttled down, a lithe blur of black and yellow. It dropped the deer at the base of the tree and melted away into the brush.

Our *mali* attempted to goad the elephant after the cat, but it wasn't easy. The beast began trumpeting, a piercing series of blasts, and its entire body began to vibrate like a motel bed. The other *malis* came running up, and within seconds all three pachyderms were going nuts—trumpeting, purring with fright, and snapping their trunks like huge bullwhips. Our animal was unquestionably the bravest of the pack; it snapped and trumpeted terrifyingly, but plowed ahead into the jungle. The other large elephant seemed paralyzed, and its *mali* whacked it sickeningly across the skull, again and again, with a stout club. Every time he pounded the beast it wailed in protest, lifting its head back and throwing its trunk into the air. The lobes of its scalp were raw; I winced with every blow.

The beating and trumpeting and "purring" held us up for a long time, and it was strange, how frightened the elephants were of the leopard, even though the two animals aren't really enemies.

Only Teri and I saw the leopard. All through the day people told us how lucky we were. They were right, I know, but it seemed like a funny kind of luck, to see a leopard for ten seconds.

It was great to be out of the dusty, windy city, and to spend time identifying birds (there are eight hundred varieties in Nepal), but the best thing we did was spend two nights up in a *machan*. Machans are observation towers, built 25 feet above the jungle floor. Up until the first of this year people were allowed to camp in them, thus blending with the habitat after a fashion and getting to see the animals at their morning and late evening ablutions (it's dangerous to venture into the jungle on foot at those times). I had a letter from Charles McDougal, a well-known tiger researcher who lives in Kathmandu, so the warden decided to be generous. During our final two days at the park we spent about 35 hours up in the machans, playing Scrabble, smoking joints, eating tangerines and listening to the incredible range of sounds. One night a family of rhinos came to bathe in a nearby waterhole, throwing themselves into the activity with gusto as peacocks cried from surrounding trees. Early in the morning we saw a group of nine spotted deer, who paused in their transit to watch, fascinated, at another bevy of peacocks walking through the grassy meadow. It was quite endearing to watch the deer watching the birds ... I guess even the wild animals themselves aren't immune to the curiosities we experience. The following morning a huge buck—this one a brown samba deer— emerged from the trees and watched us for a long while. Altogether, our journey to Chitwan was very soft-hearted, very enriching. The more I explore its variety of moods and landscapes, the more I love Nepal.

Times with Teri have gone the whole crazy range. When she arrived back here after Sri Lanka we had something of a second honeymoon; but down in Chitwan something in me went sour for a while, and I've been trying to recapture the high times without much success. My mood swings are mysterious to me, and anathema to her ... when we're on it's a wonderful thing for us both, but when I loose the groove everything becomes awkward and I sink into a kind of arrogant judgmentalism, finding fault with her every move. She remains a compassionate constant, not understanding but loving nonetheless. I observe myself and my heart fills with empathy for her. Sometimes the feeling is enough to move me to tears.

It all goes by so fast. New black leather; toothpaste wrapped in fish-printed rice paper; proof sheets and crumbs in plastic bags, wilted flowers, infected tick bites, stacks of slit envelopes. It goes by like a constellation, leaving little streaks of light on the agar. Distance, time and circular motion, I turn my head and barely have time to mutter, "Huh?" before nine months have passed. I've been in Nepal nine months, still no magnum opus out of me, and the end in sight. The "end," of course, is an abstract phenomenon: the vertex where novelty wears thin and restlessness crosses. I sit here in my eternal hotel room listening to the eternal Debussy as the eternal Teri showers, feeling like the only thing around with a leash on. Constantly haunted by the scattering of my vector, those round compulsions that drove me out here in the first place. Long ago realized I cannot force the novel, but determined to leave here with at least half-a-dozen good short stories. Limitation does have its benefits, as we deadline-draggers know. But your impression of my craft as "fleet of foot" is badly off the mark. From this end, it feels like trying to hop up the down escalator with both feet tied together.

There are no lack of ideas for short stories. What is lacking is the discipline to sit myself down at the typewriter four or five hours a day and make all the necessary mistakes.

Been eating time as a series of hors d'oeuvres. The Chitwan trip; a hike with Teri yesterday up to Nagarot, on the Kathmandu Valley's northern rim (great views of the whole Himalaya); another short trek in the offing before she goes. We wanted to be back in town for tomorrow, which is *Shivaratri*, one of the holiest and most amazing Hindu holidays of the year. Shiva devotees, dressed in yellow robes and carrying tridents, have been pouring into Kathmandu from all over Asia and converging on the temple of Pashupati, along the holy Bagmati River (which becomes the Ganges when it enters India.). Tomorrow they'll fast and perform all manner of penitence at the sacred ground, and I'll be there with my tape-recorder to lap some of it up for you. Ought to be good. Some of these guys have *crawled* here from a thousand miles off; some will be showing off their unimaginable self-mutilations. My friend Rick saw one fellow who had been cutting off a little part of his arm every year for decades, meditating devotedly as the stump tried to heal. There are a lot of crazy people in Asia, and many will be at Shivaratri.

Strong feelings of disconnection, of doing things for the sake of doing them. Raking the leaves for material. Took some (very weak) acid the other day, and bike/hiked with a group of friends up to a hilltop temple. Grasping for distinctive occurances. Admiring the wood-carvings. Trembling with the drug's exaggerated electricity and finding myself cast in a typical social drama with friends *here*. You have to give up your solitary pride in order to fit in. Felt myself being broken down, gently teased, and I realized anybody who's around me long enough ends up getting my number. Slinking back to the false humility, like the leopard who dropped his kill. Learning when to keep my mouth shut, when people have had enough of me. Surely you remember. We stood atop the thousand-year-old bricks at Changunarayan and I realized I wasn't the scout leader. Just a thin man, a wise guy, shadow like a Q-tip, lips as dry as dust, getting lost in the discolorations of Teri's sidelong glance, a gaunt grin. A direction looking for a kinetic shift. Motion in search of acceleration. You know the model. Where, and when, will I get some work done? Here, before I dare to leave. It's come to threats.

Twenty to eight and time to eat. Maybe in the pissy-smelling place tonight. Maybe out for mock-pizza. Skunk meat, or beef at the Mona Lisa with the beggars watching through the window. Love and illusion. Kathmandu, Nepal, still draws the late-night voodoo from me, that keen of incense and animal, the shitty gutters gleaming in the moonlight, like some sniffling epileptic chant that builds in my nostrils and bloats my stomach, sends me into the night with teeth and a flopping cock. Seven inches in, I pulse and squirm in the tight horn of the yoni of Asia, trying to forget the timing, trying to leap past the point of no return. It's too late for Nepal, much as I love it. Late in the twentieth century, and ain't nobody ain't aware of just how late it is. So what do I write about? The things that change, or the things that stay the same?

FEBRUARY 29

Waving and waving, this day of a thousand flags. At the sacred temple of Pashupatinath, where Teri and I will be headed in a few hours, tens of thousands of pilgrims and mendicants perform their ablutions to Lord Shiva. Men wrapped in yellow, smeared with ash, bent into impossible yogic postures. The air heavy with *ganja,* laced with incense and repetitive meditative mumblings. Letters to Shiva.

I'll be there, searching for my Muse. I can't tell if she left because she needed a vacation, or because she was tired of being ignored. At any rate the past few weeks have seen me at an ebb, accomplishing very little save the flattening of my laurels and feeling decidedly inferior. Something inside me's terribly dammed up, and rather than resign (and relax) I keep chipping away, waiting for the fissure that'll split the nucleus of it.

Suffering from the same old lack of passion. Teri notwithstanding my feelings for her, which have certainly deepended as the result of our Asian travels, exist independent from my compulsions about writing. To put it more succinctly, I'm arrested at different levels with the two ostensible "loves of my life." Can't help but feel ironic when I say I'm not feeling "fresh." I always thought getting older would mellow me, but the fact is that, when I'm not working, it's harder on me than ever.

Yet I persist in pissing time away, noting with envy—and alarm—the projects of my compatriots. Especially painful have been my encounters with a friend named Andy, who has just finished writing a short novel set in Nepal. My glimpses at the first draft have been humbling, to say the least. My tough personal goals for this voyage were supposed to yield equally tasty fruit, but unless I more or less force myself into it I'll leave here with a handful of dust for the gold coins I packed in.

One thing I've learned this past year is that I can make resolutions 'til I'm blue in the face. I can glide through the brief spells when everything seems perpetually possible, confident the feeling will last long enough to allow me to begin work "tomorrow." Another thing I've learned is that my sense of discipline isn't strong enough to threaten me effectively. The *Islands* story got out, well-wrought and on time, only because of an *external* force. Now, what is this bullshit supposed to mean? That I won't write fiction until I'm paid in advance?

"I'd leave tomorrow if it would help you to write," says Teri, and her compassionate offer makes my eyes brim with tears. If I thought it would help me to write I would ask her to leave; but the truth is that it's not a question of whether she stays or goes. It's not an external thing, although my conviction that it is was enough to drive me out here in the first place. It's an infernal internal laziness, a blockage, a cop that stops my ideas in mid-dream and sends them back as "not enough, not rich enough, not real enough, not important enough." Then someone like Andy comes along, and I ask myself if I've had my eyes open at all.

*

*(Later)*

The most remarkable thing that happened yesterday evening was my long contemplation of a burning body. The tiny-looking corpse is wrapped in white cloth, sprinkled with red *tika* powder and placed gently upon the piled wood. Straw is heaped around the base, and set aflame by an ember picked from a brazier surrounded by ganja-smoking saddhus. I watched as the straw burned away, and then the cloth, until the flesh was charring and smoking. A foot broke off and threatened to tumble from the pyre; at one point something inside the corpse burst, and a jet of wine-red blood came spurting from the depths of the flames. Teri watched in fascination; she has a sort of phobia of fire. I wanted someone to take a photo of the cremation with Teri and me kissing in the foreground, but couldn't work up the nerve.

Away from the burning ghats, up the forested hill above Pashupatinath Temple, monkeys skittered over the roofs of shrines and over the stone rows of *lingams*—Shiva phalluses. Crowds thronged below, by the sacred river, and a huge line led toward the inner sanctum ("For the Hindus Only"), wherein sits Nandi, an enormous golden bull, mount of Lord Shiva. As beautiful as the chaos was the commercial aspect of the event—stalls selling day-glo tika powder in acid colors, wreaths of mustard and colored silk puff-balls, row after row of those garish, distinctive god-and-goddess portraits as per *Are You Experienced?*, men thronging around stalls selling candy-colored bras, women sorting through bins of plastic tikas. You see a million inimitable color combinations, a thousand intricate interplays of form and material, and try to capture a bare fraction of it with your camera. But nothing else on earth but direct experience could make you know what those holy bazaars are like, or how the electricity runs through the visiting barbarian like a cosmic pipe-cleaner.

My situation: I'm a tourist again. In other words, my official visa to Nepal has expired, and as of my return to the Kingdom March 26 I am left with three months only to bring to fruition anything that might want to ripen in me. Three months, as you know, is nothing, and a pervading sense of franticness is creeping into me like mold into a long-stored loaf of Wonder Bread.

It'll cover a lot of ground if I tell you that Teri is leaving in two days. Had a weird dream last night in which she and I were parting in the middle of a dark and rolling desert (much like the one we explored in Rajasthan); I woke up in tears, held her tight. As much as I value the prospect of a few months of solitude, it seems incredible that her presence will have vanished by the weekend. Definitely leaves a void in my heart. Altogether, I'm surprised that her enormously protracted visit turned out as well as it did. We made plenty of explorations together, shared stiffling rooms and salubrious lakes, generally had an awful lot of fun. But I still feel the longing for that lonely solitude that Rilke writes of, for the lack of distraction and even loving concern that glows as it drains. To put it simply, it's hard to concentrate when there's a soul-mate around. So. Teri leaves for Burma the thirty first, and the next few days will see much rush and sadness. I'm stealing these hours for you.

But you're not really interested in all this romantic and mushy claptrap, are you? You want to hear about India. Well, I wish I had the energy to regale you with about three pages of adventures, but India sapped me and I'm still on the slow boat to recovery. To provide a minor sum of highlights: the object of our journey was to explore Rajasthan, "The land of Kings," the part of India you think about when you think turbans and camels and veils, wells in the desert, women in fire-colored saris passing beneath pink sandstone gates with ceramic jugs piled on their heads; when you think of maharajas in their spiked-gate fortresses and pavilions of marble mosaic.

The highlight of the trip as a whole was our visit to Jaisalmer. If you find it on the map of India you'll see that it's pretty much the end of the line. In that unbelievable ancient city of golden sandstone, rising out of the desert like a sandcastle, we hired camels and took a three-day trek into the heat of the Thaar. It wasn't an experience that photos could really convey—those endless (and painful!) hours of bouncing on the hump, the clear, cool nights sleeping on the sand, the abandoned villages eroded by generations of winds into forms closer to Capitol Reef than to thriving human oases. Our days were divided into long stretches of riding broken up by stops at isolated, fascinating ports-of-call. A range of sand dunes here; a green oasis lake surrounded by cattle and camel-ranchers; a huge temple slumping in the midst of ruined adobes and dry wells. Jaiselmer itself is nearly as gritty and breathtaking as the desert, and we spent long hours wandering through the cavernous Fort and along windy, dry back streets full of begging kids and shit and camels.

On March 17, Jaisalmer went temporarily insane for the holiday called *Holi*. It was celebrated with particular frenzy in Jaisalmer. Holi is the one day when the Indians can give vent to their repressed spontaneity and sexuality. Traditionally the festivities consist of men and women, lovers and otherwise, sprinkling red *tika* powder over each other and squirting all in sight with jets of colored water. Men sing ribald songs as the gals giggle in the balconies, throwing vases of color onto them, dying everything and everyone with bright colors.

Okay, that's the tradition. These days Holi is a meleé, a Mardi-Gras of florescent insanity. To step out into the streets is to be attacked by mobs and drenched with every color of the rainbow, to become a canvas for the maddened inspirations of a thousand entranced Jackson Pollacks. You can imagine me in the riotous fray of it, clutching my Nikon wrapped in a shirt and wheeling around to catch most of it on and down my back. Teri and I and every person in that Arabian Nights town looked like we'd been put in a washer with the circus troupe's non-colorfast wardrobe. Red, green, blue, purple, yellow, orange, and white from head to toe—in our ears, up our noses and, in poor Teri's case, ground into her eyes by one of the many assholes who take advantage of the holiday to molest Western gals. As you can imagine, the Indian women like to stay clean, and the chickenshit Indian men are more interested in copping a quick feel with a blonde than celebrating with their uptight townfolk. As you see, it was a giddy and sweet/sour experience. Teri got so badly mauled that even now, a dozen shampooings later, the pink remains in her hair like some failed New Wave streak job. I saved my T-shirt to show you when I get home. It was one of the most extraordinary festivals I've ever witnessed.

Many other adventures. An excellent time in Jaipur, "The Pink City", where they filmed *The Far Pavillions*; a few days in Mount Abu, a bizarre Indian hill station which is actually a resort for honeymooners, featuring such hotels as the "Hilltone" and "Sheratone." It's like Niagara Falls without the falls, or Atlantic City without the midway (or the city, for that matter). In the evenings every couple in the place flocks to romantic Sunset Point, massed together in truest Indian fashion to enjoy the solitude. Oddly, Abu is also a very holy and spiritual place... there are some very famous Jain temples there, which are said to be some of the most astonishingly beautiful and intricate marble-work in the world, surpassing in some respects even the Taj Mahal. I can only agree unhesitatingly. Another one of these places where my mouth just dropped open.

Sitting in my new (and hopefully final) house in Kathmandu, dressed in a rather absurd outfit: shorts, a YMHA T-shirt, and a powder-blue fraternity sweater that might have been appropriate on someone like Hugh Hefner twenty years ago. Feeling bizarre and twisted up for a number of reasons, but I think the main problem is that, for the first time in Nepal, I actually have some malevolent parasite in my system that requires vigilant medical treatment. Not one to be lured by pharmaceutical ways I consulted an *ayurvedic* (i.e., naturopathic) doctor, who, after feeling about my intestinal region, determined that I am suffering from a case of amoeba. He prescribed an appropriate medicine, a powder resembling licorice in odor and ground feces in appearance, to be mixed with water and wailed down three times daily. I had been doing so, nose held, for the past two days, until by accident or unconscious design, I forgot the foul packet after using it last night in a nearby Italian restaurant. As today is a holiday the restaurant is closed. So about a half hour ago I decided to go for the gusto and begin a course of a new, different, and decidedly western cure, a pill called Amelast. Having taken my first two of these white lozenges I feel the onset of indescribable but uncomfortable side effects, and wonder when and if this hodge-podge of eastern medicine-meets-western medicine will cure me. Loathe to patronize the greedy foreign medics and distrusting all doctors, I fire blindy at the parasites with an arsenal of herbs and chemicals, figuring that at any rate the amoebas ought to feel pretty unwelcome by now and might well take the hint.

*

Returned March 27 from Rajasthan, a very intense and colorful three-week trip highlighted by a three-day camel trek into the Thaar desert. With bright orange turban, sly Jewish grin and Walkman, I resembled more a Rajneesh-nik than Lawrence of Arabia. Teri was likewise attired, add designer sunglasses. Regardless of our ludicrous appearance it was a wonderful trek—the desert so vast and quiet, so full of rocks and ruins and scattered with lush oases.

But the desert was also cruel. Though trees and thistles abounded, the overwhelming impression was of sand and stones. The sand like a hot, malevolent powder, ranging in color from scab-purple to a parched umber; the stones in all forms, of all descriptions. Sometimes they baked on the ground like flat iron plates; sometimes they gashed upward, as sharp and misshapen as petrified coral. It was incredible to think that this thirsty landscape was once an ocean floor....Still, there were signs: shale impressed with undulating ripple marks; a boy by the cenotaphs selling round little fossils.

During the long, jarring ride I had considerable time to debate which was in greater pain—my ass or my feet. The latter won out. When we stopped to pick up some firewood I discovered that the mean iron stirrups had chafed my feet so badly they were bleeding. I rode from that point on with my feet hanging loose, which increased the jarring on my ass-bone but was preferable to the destruction of my arches.

The desert was desert in all directions. Nothing but low shrubbery and horizon for 360 degrees. The stones every color of metal and vulcanized metal and metal lotuses, like opaline mushrooms on the sand.

My driver—who I quickly christened "The Kid"—never shut up. He was obviously in love with me, with camels, with the desert, with the sound of his own voice, and kept up a constant stream of babble and song punctuated lavishly with hugs, histrionics and the monosyllabic query, "Good?! Good?!" Every time insisting upon the answer, then repeating that three or four times. Whenever deer run across the stony hills he would lapse into ecstasies of vocalization, grabbing me by the throat, pointing to the terrified creatures and howling, "Look! Look! Oh, yes, good! Very good! Very very good! Safari very good! Hello! Yes! Look! Hello!" and so on. It was amusing, contagious, unnerving, obnoxious.

Lunch typically consisted of biscuits, tea, and a greenish porridge that looked as close to shit as anything I'd ever tried to swallow. We ate what we could and threw the rest to the dogs.

I developed no empathy for camels. In fact, I grew to loathe them more each passing day. They're incredibly ugly and stupid; their voices sound like a well gurgling about six gallons of snot. The worst thing, though, is their smell—they fart incessantly, and it astonishes me that any plant or shrub growing on the good Earth could be processed into so overpoweringly foul an odor. You never get used to it. Every time I caught a whiff I nearly gagged, and the air was ever perfumed by the flatulent beasts. In addition, my camel had some obscene festering dampness on the back of his head. It may have been an open sore, or a mating secretion of some kind; who knows. In any case it served gratuitously as a breeding ground for flies as well. So between the sound, sight, and smell of these animals I've come to the conclusion that camels are the ugliest creatures in God's creation—at least among the mammals.

But, as I've said, the beauty and romance of the setting far outweighed the malignant idiosyncracies of the camels. It was a wonderful time.

*

Reading the *Ramayana* has been enlightening. It's a beautiful legend, and Buck's storybook approach is infectious in that it draws you in to the dazzle and power of the Age-Before-Last. I love that link between the Hindu and Buddhist worlds—Vishnu, the Preserver, returns to Earth ten times to save the world. The seventh incarnation as Rama; the eighth as Krishna; the ninth as the Buddha. And, if it's all true, the tenth—Juggernaut—will make a clean slate of it.

On our train ride from Jaisalmer to Mount Abu I took my copy of *The Essential Hemingway* from my pack. Teri and I looked for a long time at the portrait on the cover. The *Ramayana* also has a cover portrait, a reproduction from the New York Metropolitan Museum of the youthful and triumphant Rama. I held the two books side by side. The detailed, squinting rendition of Papa H. and the stylized Rama made a startling contrast. Even through the portraits were oriented toward each other—Hemingway facing right, Rama to the left—there was no eye contact between them.

"Two heroes," I remarked. "They don't see eye to eye."

"This is reality," said Teri, indicating the piercing-eyed writer, "and this is myth."

Indeed—but the two men also showed a marked difference in confidence. One had rowed himself by bleeding hands through an ocean of wounds and uncertainties; the other had plowed, equally wounded but invincible, along a predestined dharma.

"Both figures, real and imaginary, had their dharmas," observed Teri.

"And they've both become legends."

Is my great need to follow my dharma, or still to find it? Maybe I'm learning that you find it by following it.


MARCH 27

Arrived at the border after an all-day ride, cramped and aching from vinyl seats and the 'greenhouse' effect. The afternoon had been sunny—but now, at 5 P.M., it was warm and overcast. I stamped out of India and walked the two hundred yards through log-weighted checkposts to the Nepal immigration post. There was plenty of paperwork, and conversation—in Nepali—with the guards. Teri arrived just behind me. She filled out her form for a while, then, "Look at the wind."

Never seen it happen faster. Within half a minute the air was black with dust. The wind, barely a breeze a moment ago, mounted and howled through the village, throwing tornadoes of sand before it. People and animals alike ran frantically through the streets, shielding their heads against flying objects. Trees cracked. The power blacked out. As pockets of alternatingly warm and icy air gusted past the checkpost the sky exploded into webs of lightning, bursting from every direction at once, like the Fourth of July in a fog. The raw power of it all was transfixing. Gurkhas—Gurkhas!—were running for shelter, hands clasped behind their heads like surrender, into the lightless bunkers.

Every desk and chair, every stack of papers, was coated with tiny dunes.

The storm drove past with a speed to match its arrival. A band of light split at the western horizon, illuminating every tree, building and figure as if under an orange klieg light. Then the sun crept into the gap, and the gray eastern sky was filled with a dark, almost sinister rainbow. All above us, lightning continued to play across the heaven like a net upon the sea, breaking into brilliant rivulets which chased each other between the clouds. It was breathtaking and terrifying, an unfathomable omen of blessing or blame. I could not, for all my awareness of paranoid symptomology, help but feel smack in the middle of it.

The hot, pre-monsoon season is beginning. Not comfortable weather, though cooler, thank God, than India was. I got a little sick in India and lost some (more) weight, so I've been on a milk-shake binge this week. Feeling inordinately lean, though still strong and full of lists (as opposed to listless). Wolfing down the crazy, inexplicable foods you've sent. The tuna was most welcome! You can well imagine what happened to the perishables; they perished. Figs, dates, pistachios, looking rather mean after their five months at sea. And the crackers! They had fulfilled the condition of all spent life, and returned to the dust from which they had sprung. The soups and fish and peanut butter (smooth???) arrived intact, though not a single can remained undented, and the seal on the Jif was astir, as though some curious customs-man had enjoyed a taste of the exotic.

Sitting in a new room in my new house, the seventh place I've lived in Kathmandu. But this is the place I should have gotten ten months ago. No use crying over spilt *chang*; I'm here now, and will stay until the end of June, by which point I will have milked every possible visa extension from the jackals at Immigration and will be forced to follow my luggage to the airport. The next three months, I'm sure, will pass like lightning, and though I must admit the news of late has seemed to me to be downright disgusting concerning U.S. affairs both at home and abroad, I still look forward to visiting America again, and dipping from that well of possibilities before deciding, frankly, whether or not to expatriate myself. This always happens when I read Hemingway....

I'm almost afraid to write about what's happening with me. No novel, and I kick myself constantly for it, but assignments in an unending stream and the invitation to go anywhere I choose. Total mobility, though, does not but depend on one's internal gyroscope, and mine continues to wobble and skip. Too much amazement is like too much chocolate, it makes you constipated and speedy. In the midst of assignments for *Islands* and *Geo* I stagger into trenches of self-doubt, the feeling that writing for magazines is a cop-out, induced by financial seduction. Funny how it works in a loop. My excuse for not being able to settle and write (fiction) was financial straits. Now, through writing for magazines, I'm financially solvent, and wonder what my excuse will be next. Keep telling myself to shut up and take advantage of it—the joyrides to Sri Lanka, India, Java are at least worthwhile experiences, and can't help but help any future writing I do. For me, unlike you, the main enemy is laziness. That and, in my black moments, the sensation of a genuine lack of talent. But I am happy. Confused, yes, and slightly panicked by my recent birthday, but happy.

I'm no good at finding words anymore. About three inches in from your solar plexus there's a rope wound with soul and fear and primitive blood-lust thrill, a pagan bell-pull, and India just grabs that line and yanks. I want you to have the experience, but can only relate the pathos, because only at those moments of lusty terror does the experience make any cross-cultural sense. You can't imagine what it was like in that ancient palace courtyard in the Jaisalmer Fort, the air so thick with colored powders that you were breathing it, a mass of day-glo men singing and howling at the tops of their lungs as girls and women threw buckets of dye onto our heads from the balcony...but you can well imagine the moment when, as is their license on this one particular day, the delirious youths attacked Teri, rubbed gritting paste into her eyes so hard that she was reduced to near-hysteria and tears...and I, a man among men, totally into it, mixing pity with pagan fascination and wishing she'd stayed in the hotel...some part of me totally comfortable, all covered with powder and paste, never minding the painted hands as they came at me from every direction.

My long-awaited friend Kathy arrived (I'd been waiting for her since last October); the plan was that we'd take a three-week trek together. Hadn't seen the gal for six years, so neither of us really knew what to expect. What happened was that she hung around a while and finally decided to go trekking with a bunch of women instead. So she left four days ago. The whole thing stinks of fate as far as I'm concerned; something was conspiring to put me in my current situation, that is, faced with a *solo* trek—something I've known I should do, but never felt spiritually prepared for. So here's the scoop...today being Wednesday...I'm flying on Friday to the village of Tumlingtar in the far east, and heading alone up the Arun Valley toward Makalu Base Camp...then backtracking and venturing across to the Solo Khumbu region (where I went last October) for a festival called *Mani Rimdu*, which occurs the second week in May. I'm hoping the time alone will enable me to relax in my own company, enough so that the ideas that have been jammed up in me can start to flow. Sketching out ideas for a book of "Stories to Entertain God," starring the eternal Yoki Fang, human reincarnation of Buddha's horse, enjoying his first lifetime as a human and relationships with a host of other characters who've been at it a lot longer. What my muse needs is a good enema, which I'll give her on the trail. Maybe, as you suggested, I'll also give her a shave.

Time seems to be going by so fast, and I'm clinging to the pendulum. I had the usual nightmare last night—a dream that all my friends and I have recurrently—that I was back home in America, this voyage over, the transition over, just back in the States the way it always used to be and always will be, with Mom and Dad and the croissant shops and newspapers and perforated, percolated madness, sale items everywhere, light-box art and shaved pubes, movies, Oscars, avocados, hit-parades and six-packs and television sets, computers and Cabbage-Patch dolls and Jane Fonda, everyone looking for work, everyone thrashing around for inner peace, everyone scrambling for love, and me stammering in someone's living room and touching everything, trying to explain that I've just come home to visit, yeah, just for a day, I've got to leave tomorrow, of course, back to Nepal...but a goat barks outside and I wake up swallowing time in a room full of mosquitoes as the first rays of April 18th light up the eyes of Buddha on Swayambhunath, gleaming from the top of that hill...wake up in a house in the center of Kathmandu, Rick and Nancy sleeping upstairs, the maid ringing the doorbell, and I know that upstairs they're dreaming the same dreams that I just dreamt, also poised (even closer than me) to the edge of their departures.

True to intuition, things around me are flailing, slipping gears. Hey, why not? Some of it's alright and some of it's not alright, and there's a vast middle ground that might turn out alright after all. It's a blow, that Henson doesn't want to trek with me—but not worth taking personally. I've been closed up to her, I think, but maybe I was waiting to open up in the wilderness. Well, I won't know, or maybe I will. I'm that sure of things.

It's a panic, that I'll be trekking alone.

\*

So many books about the writer's struggle with God. I guess *Moby Dick* is also that much of a book. My writing now is about struggling with...style. The question is, should I write a book for the express purpose of entertaining God? The problem is, I can never decide whether to pray or masturbate. I have concluded that the two are mutually exclusive.

No wonder Kate doesn't want to spend three weeks trekking with me! No wonder that I'm terrified to spend three weeks alone with myself! I'm a gutless Ahab, alright, clinging to the sextant and blanching at the Whale.

\*

I stand up on the roof and can't read the sky. Bizarre letters from the Santa Barbara artists make me feel like an obsolete commodity. Parties, marriages, Bukowski-esque sex; I feel the rope sagging. I stand up on the roof and it sweeps over me like a wave of broken glass: I'm alone at last. "Strange travel suggestions are dancing lessons from God," writes Kurt Vonnegut, but there's something more....I stand up on the roof and realize that there is finally nothing and no one who I miss. The thought is like swallowing an icicle, but it's true.

Maybe you can see how it all ties in. All of it: the tug between dance and solitude; letters about shaving and prayer and masturbation; and especially the relationship between my letters and my journal entries, which share the same unconscious audience. Do you pick up that I've become very religious out here? All that interests me now is to write about God, and the thousand straight or scatterbrained paths to the end of the rainbow.

Life in transience. The community here is like a Slinky making its inimitable way down a flight of stairs. Down the up escalator, to repeat a metaphor. Amazing how limber you get if you travel enough; you can almost kiss your own ass goodbye as you rustle from place to place. Knowing when it's good and knowing when it's got to be over. Circular time tastes better than linear time, but this global drain-plunging is a sticky hybrid of both.

Got to close this letter now and plunge into action preparing for my trek. Nothing is easy. Heading into this day feeling clean and hungry. The air outside is full of seeds. The goats that woke me up have already been sacrificed.

*

Had a terrific Seder the evening of the 17th; mostly gentiles, even a Nepalese woman. It went smoothly, but I was a little more self-conscious than I was in Santa Barbara. It was tough to get some of the things we needed. . . . Is it kosher to use the shank bone of a non-kosher animal? (Did you know that yaks are kosher? Can you imagine my relief?) What to do if you can't get horseradish? Fortunately, our biggest problem was solved easily: a sealed package of the Genuine Item, matzoh, was donated to our cause by the Israeli Embassy.

Transculturization is a long, slow process, but the evolution continues. It's hard to be even a conservative Jew in Asia; Buddha is so magnetic that one inevitably develops a blend of beliefs. I find myself growing alarmingly eclectic, paying homage to nearly all of the Buddhist and Hindu pantheon. Not yet at the point of offering live animal sacrifices, but I do feel I qualify for the protection of the local Bosses. New skin for the old ceremony, is all. Just be good and don't worry, and if you think you're bound for below make sure to pack plenty of marshmallows.

## THE ARUN VALLEY TREK

The walk from the airstrip at Tumlingtar was a time to remember just how hot and just how painful one's first day of trekking can be. Sweat poured from me; my hips chafed, then blistered; and I had to stop at nearly every *dhaar* to cool off. This on an empty stomach, and the iodized water in my canteen seems to be making me sick.

At one point I was resting in the shade after gaining a ridge. An administrator from Biratnagar had elected to accompany me, and I apologized for my frequent breaks by explaining that I was carrying twenty kgs—a rather heavy load (he had only an umbrella). Just as I voiced this woe I saw a stout man with oriental features and shorts smiling at me. He carried an obviously expensive backpack and a strange aluminum walkingstick/umbrella combination, and wore a very impressive watch around his thick wrist.

"Oh, I don't think that's a very heavy pack!" he laughed. "Only twenty kilos? I carried forty kilos in the Falklands; and the snow was up to our knees!"

And so I made the brief acquaintance of Tej Bahadur Rai, lately of the Gurkhas, who confirmed for me that story I'd oft heard floating around: that the Argentinian soldiers fled when they learned that these Nepalese mercenaries were joining the British.

"Yes—they knew we were fighting with our khukris," said Tej Bahadur, "so their necks started itching."

Much to write and remember about yesterday and last night, and little of it good. Don't know what happened—I was seized by a brain-fever of sorts. Simultaneous with the deterioration of my mental state I experienced the onset of a physical malaise—slight nausea, extreme weariness, dizzyness, weakness. Fortunately I'd been able to hire a porter in Kanbari, because I'm not sure I could have gone on otherwise.

I seemed to feel worse as time wore on. In Kanbari people had been telling me that Bhotebas was only two hours away, but I was willing to bet this was a damned conservative estimate. Wanted to get there and rest; felt weaker with every step.

We arrived in Bhotebas after sunset. The tiny village was the home of Purbu, my porter, who put me up in his simple hut. It was quite crowded with his family. All I wanted to do was lie down and rest. I pulled out my sleeping bag to use as a pillow. But before I could get comfortable Purbu came and sat down next to me and tried to explain something. He kept touching his arm as if poking it, and saying something about a *siun*—or, as I understood it, a needle.

My outlandish interpretation of this charade was that he wanted us both to poke our arms and mingle our blood, thus becoming brothers. There was no way I was going to do this, and I plainly indicated so. But then I realized that he must have meant something else, because his wife's sister came over holding a little girl and, by way of illustrating Purbu's request, lifted up the baby's dress. The child's entire body was covered with raw second-degree burns, as if a cauldron of boiling oil had splattered over her. Purbu confirmed that this exact thing had happened five days before.

Talk about a feeling of impotence! What could I do? In a pathetic gesture of compassion I took out my first aid powder and gave the little girl a liberal salting. She cried piteously. Aside from that symbolic act, I could only advise the mother to get her child post-haste to the clinic in Kanbari for treatment. If those wounds get infected, she's finished.

The family went into the main room to cook dinner, and I lay down. My condition deteriorated almost at once. I fell into a fitful half-sleep, shaking uncontrollably as cold and hot flashes racked through me. Hugging myself into fetal position I seriously considered descending back to Tumlingtar the next morn, and ending this thankless solo trek. The fantasy approached certainty during dinner. I couldn't eat, and thought for sure I'd keel right over. Finally I had to excuse myself and crawl into bed, too hot, too cold, nauseous and very lonely.

Felt better in the morning. God knows why. You better believe I prayed last night . . . but what caused it all? I have a couple of theories. Maybe heat-shock; maybe culture-shock; maybe even withdrawal from the hash I smoked in Kathmandu, although I certainly don't crave the stuff. At any rate I got an early start this morning, and now sit in Chichila, halfway to Ururus, forcing down the eggs and *dhal* and *tarkari*. I still feel bad in my soul, but it'll pass once I can eat a little bit of time.

*

The path down from Num to the river was long and steep but very sweet. The sounds of the Arun rose and faded as I rounded switchbacks and gingerly toe-stepped down rocky stairs. I thought about whether the trip would be better different or worse different if Dorje, the new porter-cum-lama I hired in Ururus, wasn't behind me—that is, if I were really alone. A porter and guide is necessary now, but I'm looking forward to next week, when I solo it over the pass and into the Solo Khumbu.

Dorje lagged considerably far behind, and I stopped often to admire the spectacular butterflies that stooped and flitted alongside the path: black swallowtails with yellow, white or blue markings, and an astonishingly gorgeous red-white-black variety. I might as well admit it—the butterflies had me thinking about Teri, and wondering why I've picked this solo trip to be in such a romantic mood.

Those thoughts dilapidated when I espied a rather amazing sight among the trees: a tangle of wrist-thick metal cable, seamless, at least 100 meters long and weighing, by my naive estimation, around 10 kg the meter.

When I reached the river—a powerful but visually unspectacular torrent—I realized at once that the cable had been hauled in with an eye to constructing a new bridge. It's direly needed; the old one is a menace! Long as life, six inches wide, floored with matchstick planks and suspended by rusted, pencil-thin cables, it swayed nauseatingly as a couple of terrified Sherpanis made their way across. My transit was characterized by outward calm and inward trepidation. Not only was the bridge every second seeming closer to collapse, but as the Arun roared dizzily below I got the illusory impression that the bridge itself was racing, hell-bent, in the opposite direction—much like a building, seen before a sea of receding clouds, appears to be toppling forward onto the viewer.

It was nothing but up from the Arun. Walking alone, slowly but surely, I opened my mind to whatever thoughts came hobbling along. The usual array dominated—it's incredible, how many times I can add the figures that comprise Dorje's salary, subtract the days that define this half-hearted trek, or count the weeks until I see Teri. But that ain't all—just as an infinite number of monkeys at an infinite number of typewriters will eventually pen the greatest works of philosophy, so will my brain stir up a worthwhile notion, given world enough and time. What I realized while climbing to Saartang is this: this solo trek is the *direct physical parallel* of what I must be prepared to do after I return to Kathmandu. Hard work and solitude, as mental as this trek is physical. This three-week journey into an unthreatening wilderness must model mid-May's future. So bon voyage, buddy—and amen.

APRIL 25

Going up; really up. Like Adam's Peak, it seemed it would never end. But it wasn't really difficult; just lifting one leg, and then the other, we climbed each successive switchback, bound for the ominous fog. Another endless stair, with every pause an arbitrary "floor."

Flowers began to appear—small white and purple ones, then fabulously fragrant violets, lavender, and, high in the mists, the rhododendrons. Subtle touches of them—red, lilac, they emerged from the clouds.

A dream-stroll. Damp climbs over stones, the air perfumed. Sometimes we'd come across little meadows, the entrances marked by prayer-flags; sometimes we'd break through onto ridges, and I'd drop my jaw at the scale of it all. The depth of the valleys, the speed of the mist, the rivers of snow on the mountains beyond, revealed during the too-brief partings of the clouds. It was all so very different from anything I had expected.

We reached a ridge-top meadow of dry silver grasses and sparse, wiry shrubs. A few rhododendron bushes added color. The sun came out just as we arrived, and it was suddenly so hot that I took off both my shirts. This was Kang Ma Dhara, our destination, at 13,000 feet. After a few minutes of sunlight we were completely enveloped in mist, so that it seemed as if our ridge was The Only Place, an island in an ocean of clouds. A few waterholes; one in particular very small, very clear. All things became possible. It was very cold.

I set up the tent, but had to relocate it because the ground had a barely visible slope that could not not ignored from a horizontal perspective. Moved it to a flat, slightly damp clearing. Then I made a "doorstep" of some flat stones, sat on them, and had a little taste of smoke; my first on the trek so far. One strong hit. Then I began to set up a small breakfast campfire by my tent. It was at that point that the egg began to crack.

Dorje was out collecting wood. I wandered off, very high indeed, to explore the water holes, and returned with several full containers. It occurred to me that I ought to record every detail, every move I made, every subtle nuance of the landscape. Brought up one jug of pool water and one of snow water to see if I could taste the difference. A slight twist of earth in the former.

I squatted down, filled my little cooking-pot and stood up. An overwhelming rush washed over me, like a thousand dreams at once. I staggered forward on automatic pilot, thinking, What next? Where am I?

Alone. Alone, with Dorje. Alone and the Earth like a rolled-out carpet.

"You can be alone," I said out loud. "You can be alone anywhere, you can be great if you want, but even if you're afraid to be great you can still be whole."

After getting a few things together at the tent I came down to the main fire-site. I staggered to behold the enormous pile of logs Dorje had collected with his *khukuri*. It was more than I could even lift. My admiration was boundless, and I told him so—but then I began to wonder how good an idea it was to chop down all that wood. The feeling of satisfaction changed abruptly into one of extreme guilt, like I'd planned this trek with my head up my ass. When he wandered off and began hacking away at a rhododendron tree, I protested. "Dorje, we already have enough wood to last a week." He looked at me like I was nuts. "All trekking groups cut down tree," he explained.

We made tea and cooked dinner. The photo of the Swayambhunath Buddha served as our mascot and protector. I made ramen noodles with onions, and opened a can of salmon; Dorje cooked *dhalbaht*. We turned the pots black.

The sun is down, and the distant mountains preceding the Kanchenjunga range no longer glow. Dorje squats by the fire like Frodo in his gray sweater and black woolen poncho; I in my flannel, down and wool. It's getting bloody cold, and too dark to write, but let me say this: I've waited all my life to feel this good.

Kitimbo and I found a great place. We were originally going to stay in Pikuuwa, along the Arun, and that would've been enough—but there was no one home at the single shack, hence we were obliged to climb another three hours through the damp, hanging jungle, exhausted to the limit, to find Yaphu. This house is a real score. The *didi* is smart-looking; she reminds me of a young, Nepali version of Golda Meir.

Our location: high on a ridge on the right bank of the Arun, surrounded by plants and trees, anyone's idea of a jungle. But it's cool—clouds low all around the hills, intermittent rain, the ever-present distant rumbling of thunder, a stiff, humming breeze through the plantains. Chicks chirping. I involuntarily recall last night, and Kitimbo butchering the rooster: one minute alive and squawking; the next dead and plucked; the next, hacked into still warm pieces. They work fast around here.

A day of many impressions, spent mostly mindlessly, alongside the mighty Arun or crossing its lively tributaries on rude bridges. So much of Nepal looks the same, trek to trek, but the spirit and quality of the people changes. And the flow of feelings, when I open up to curiosity, is ever changing but eternally positive. It feels good to climb; it feels good to rest. I enjoy trekking with Kitimbo, who is more of a pure presence than was Dorje—he's tough and maybe a bit less cosmopolitan, but allows me more privacy and time for contemplation.

One thing I never want to forget about this Arun trek is the insect life—the spectacular bugs. Saw a butterfly today with yellow polka-dotted purple patches on its suede-brown wings, that seemed it had just emerged from the looking-glass. What else needs to be remembered? The fine gray and purple sand as we boulder-hopped along the Arun; the balsa terraces gleaming in the low light, against steel-gray mists; the way the sky blinks with lightning, as if some important personage had appeared beyond the hill to a flurry of flash photos. And now a huge bale of hay comes walking up the trail, easily eight times the size of the boy carrying it.

No matter how depressed the days begin, they all seem to find their peaks. For every mountain mist...no doubt in my mind that I'm heading for Namche, and very much looking forward to crossing the Salpa Pass and entering the Khumbu region. Given good weather, I'll be in Phedi in two days. At Salpa in three.

End of the chase. The hare's bounding off into the rain; he can have it. Maybe I'm trying to feel good about a bad decision, or trying to feel bad about a good decision. I don't know. At any rate my plans have changed.

All morning, the cheerful *"Aja puukchha!"* (Today is enough!) came in response to our queries about whether or not we could make Phedi by nightfall. By afternoon these changed into the ambiguous *"Aja puukhola,"* and when the weather changed to pouring rain we at last encountered the fatal *"Aja puukchaina!"* Yet we drove on. At least we could *see* Phedi ahead of us—it looked like a town right out of *Lord of the Rings,* up on a high hillside beyond the Irkuwa Kola. We knew if we pressed we could make it. Rain dripped off my Kelty pack, soaking the button of the King of Nepal I'd fixed on, and ran off the brim of my hat. Workers came running from the fields with baskets over their heads. We met a man cowering under a water-buffalo pen.

*"Phedi, aja puukchha?"*

*"Puukchaina!"*

Kitimbo pointed to the mythical city high on the distant hill.

*"Tyo gaon Phedi ho?"* ("Is that town Phedi?")

*"Phedi hoina!"* the man shouted ("No, it's not Phedi!") and continued in Nepali, "Phedi is *high!"* He then rattled off a stream of directions that fell upon our spirits like hail. But we went on, somewhat half-heartedly.

We found a bunch of people by a big, slanting black rock, baskets down, taking shelter from the rain, and decided to join them. The conversation may someday bear recounting in its entirety, but the salient bits of information we gleaned were that: the bridge was down; there was no longer any real path visible through the jungle up to Phedi; the 4,000 foot climb from Phedi to the Salpa Pass was barely discernable, except by the notch of the pass itself, which was a meter deep in snow; it hadn't stopped raining for "all days"; and, by account of one old woman's brilliant pantomime, "the leeches will suck your balls dry."

Along came a couple of young teachers from Phedi, both carrying umbrellas and radios. They pulled out their cigarettes, I pulled out my map, and we had a lively and mutually incomprehensible conversation about the future fate of Hong Kong. Our little chat inevitably turned to Phedi, the road thereto, and neither fellow could recommend it for either spectacular scenery or pleasant walking. One of the men, in fact, was very direct.

"You will not succeed," he said in English. It seemed odd to me that he knew this particular phrase.

It took a long time to decide what to do. I could hardly bring myself to turn around, so deeply ingrained is that nosedive toward conflict. The thought of pain is not that alarming to me, but I had to ask, "why bother?" And why bother indeed, if you can't enjoy it. It's the old myth that things get realer as they get harder. But more and more the weather was grating on me, like a recurrent bad dream. "Let's head back to Tumlingtar," I said to Kitimbo, feeling as if I'd just bitten down on a dried, salted plum.

But the rest of the afternoon bore me out. We slouched toward Dingla, sinking and slipping on the muddy trails. Back toward Phedi it looked even worse—and impenetrable sea of gray, the river roaring forth. A couple of times we had to duck under trees, or into the shelter of houses; it became disorienting. I lost all sense of direction.

The sun's down now, and our trial-by-rain is over. At the moment I'm sitting on the porch of a stilted Rai house in Mrajuuwa, surrounded by kids and staring up the green thighs of the valley into the dark, saturated crotch of the Irkuwa River, thanking the Lord that I had the sense to turn away from that mess.

MAY 2

Signing on—for another week. Fate works in strange ways; strange travel suggestions are still, as Kurt Vonnegut asserts, "dancing lessons from God." And, eternally, there are the mountain mists, and mountain scenes. Like the stark, bold peaks sheltering Panch Pokhari, the Five Lakes, this morning's sharp weather affirmed how right this is.

I feel a hell of a lot better than I did yesterday, and am looking forward to exploring the Arun's 'restricted' northern regions, home of the Bhotiya clans. I've sacrificed the grueling for the fascinating, and that's always a fair trade in my book.

It took some doing, but most of the obstacles I had to overcome were in myself. The momentum carrying me back toward Kathmandu was strong and ugly. It required a peculiar set of circumstances to defeat: stumbling into the Royal Nepal Airlines office before I even knew we were in Tumlingtar; the wonderfully encouraging clerk there; Kitimbo's ever-diligent presence, saving me from utter physical exhaustion; and the hapless, eager police officer, content with a very small "fee." In the end I was able to get a permit, and decided: go for it. And so I am.

The one big question now is Kitimbo. Think I'll pay him off tomorrow morning, and continue on toward Hatiya, Honngoan and the restricted areas alone. I've got only one more week, and I want it to be—pure.

MAY 6
*Hatiya, Nepal*

The fantastic round-trip to Honngoan is over. It was the peak of this trek, the closest I've been to what is truly unspoiled in this country. Feeling very happy and satisfied—some elements of my spiritual expectations for this entire trek have at last been fulfilled.

The day began beautifully clear. Brilliant, once the sun came up. The surrounding mountains were all visible—not the ice-white Himals I'm used to, but the snow-streaked peaks to the east, and part of Popti-la, which serves as the pass from Chipuwa into Tibet. Walked around, took some photos, and found the lama who makes hats. It's been an obsession of mine to buy a lama-hat in Hatiya, and this was one of the day's early successes. The next was meeting Sarod, a young local official with a terrific smile, who offered to "chaperone" me along the trail above Hatiya, to the forbidden village of Honngoan.

Thought I'd had a good breakfast—a fried-egg sandwich and coffee—but to my grotesquely expanded stomach it was barely an hors d'oeuvre. Thus did we embark on the 1,000-meter uphill hike, Sarod dressed in his official finery, I in shorts and a thermal shirt, protective *yantrs* around my neck, stomach growling and ballooning. It was an astonishing lovely walk. We climbed high above the Arun, and the rooftops of Hatiya condensed into a thatched hive of bamboo and tin. As we gained altitude the river became a silver slice far below, twisting hard east before elbowing north again. The rest stops were decorated with *mani* walls, their stones carved with benevolent mantras.

We climbed through a jungle-path so dark and quiet that it seemed to be the place where all dreams begin and end. Emerging, we came upon the first of the distinctly Bhotiya, or Bon Po, *mani* walls. Now the mantras and prayer-wheels were painted in bright primaries, and color-striped prayer-flags fluttered atop bamboo stalks. Finally we climbed through an earthslide, up the side of a steep hill filled with goats and sheep, and found ourselves sitting by a majestic arrangement of mani-stones and prayer-flags, the wind whistling, the otherworldly village of Honngoan spread out before us with a relaxed cadence.

The road led straight ahead, on a clear trail banked with green, past stone shrines and fences, the entire valley panorama soaring above and below to the north and east. Far on the upriver hills, the path to Chipuwa rose into the clouds. The sky was lowering; it seemed all of Honngoan lay perhaps a hundred feet beneath the belly of an enormous cloudbank.

A stiff breeze kept the prayer-flags alive. I love those flags; it occurred to me to ask Sarod if I might get a few of them in Honngoan itself, and he agreed that it might be possible. We elected to try.

We journeyed deeper into town. Many of the houses had stone monuments propped up out front. "For dharma," explained Sarod, for I guessed they might be gravestones.

There was a small courtyard with a mani-wall and a few blacksmiths at work. We stopped here in order to speak with a middle-aged man sitting on the ground. He looked uncannily western, dressed in a seedy nylon parka and sneakers, like a cross between Peter Falk and Alan Arkin. It took a while for it to sink in, but I finally realized that this was the village lama. The moment he saw my camera he began besieging me to take his photo—his gestures were so histrionic, so comical, so desperate, that I had to laugh. He reminded me of a drunk uncle at a wedding who jumps at any chance to get into the picture. Or of myself, anywhere. Uncertain of how seriously to take this erstwhile religious figure I lumbered about in mental confusion—until the scene suddenly improved upon itself.

With a barrage of roars and hollers, a second lama strode drunkenly into the courtyard. He staggered in on bow-legs, a furious look in his eyes, one hand gripping the hilt of his sheathed sword. Face screwed up into a mask of fury he raged up to Sarod, shouting angry words into his face. He then turned upon me, shouting louder, and pulled his sword from its holster—brandishing the black, razor-sharp weapon above my head. The first lama looked on with amused approval.

This maniac was apparently the first lama's apprentice; a junior lama, perhaps in his mid-twenties. Sarod grabbed his sword-arm and calmed the man down, but the junior lama kept shouting and, reaching awkwardly into the pocket of his jacket, pulled out what was either an official letter or notice of some kind. It was the most dog-eared document I have laid eyes on, but it seemed of the greatest imaginable import, for the lama waved it threateningly in Sarod's face and pointed, death in his eye, at me.

I couldn't read the notice, but Sarod did. He shook his head, laughed, and said something in the hill tongue that caused the crowd—by now a substantial mob was present—to break into laughter. I got the feeling it was something very simple, like "You have the wrong man." In any case, his words clearly defused the situation, and the sword returned to its sheath.

Sarod said a few more things and we moved on. I wasn't sure where we were heading, but I hoped it had something to do with getting those prayer-flags.

"Hey!" I remarked gleefully to Sarod. *"Ali kaati rakshi laggio, ho?"* ("Those guys were a little bit drunk, yes?")

"HO!" he responded with hoarse mirth, and I turned around to see his famous grin. But Sarod wasn't behind me—the junior lama was! Sarod was behind him, followed by the other lama. I suddenly understood the obvious: any attempt to find local prayer-flags would needs begin and end with the lamas.

Onward we wandered. I must admit I was somewhat apprehensive about the situation. The lamas lived in a higher part of town—"Honngoan Heights"—and getting there required negotiating a narrow path cut inside the unstable bowl formed by a massive landslide. The drunken lamas were never silent, but encouraged us onward with shouts (delivered in the sub-informal Nepalese one might use on a herd of goats), and by stumbling into us from behind. They refused to walk ahead of us, rightfully afraid that we would not follow.

Arriving at their house, the lamas continued their antics. By this point their human audience had grown by a couple of *didis*. These, ostensibly the wives or mothers of the two, seemed to be thoroughly enjoying the situation.

The junior lama moved to a corner, where he picked up a twin-headed drum and a sort of ritual spear. This was a long wooden rod with a sharp metal point, crowned at the opposite end by a pair of wire "horns." Issuing a mighty roar he plunged this spear deeply into the floorboards, with such force that his pants fell almost to his knees. Then, slowly but with amazing drunken grace, he performed a meditative, chanting dance around the upright spear, seemingly unconscious of his pants edging down to his ankles.

His master watched with a rapt smile from his seat on the floor, calling at me every few minutes to fetch my camera out. Unfortunately, the room was far too dark for photographs. I didn't know whether what I was watching was a complete charade or true religion, but took a cue from the fact that the *didis* were no longer laughing. In fact, they were watching with deep interest.

At one point the head lama got up and pulled his friend's pants back up. This had no effect upon the rhythm of the performer, who continued to prance around the erect spear, shaking his drum to an almost painfully slow cadence and punctuating the dance with throaty shouts. His pants came down again. This time the teacher just pulled them off altogether. I wondered if he was wearing anything else up inside his cloak, and my answer arrived directly. The lama let loose a loud exclamation and stomped decisively forward, and down came his boxer shorts.

I was suddenly convinced that this apprentice lama was performing a mysterious, shamanistic strip-tease, working his clothes off his body by pure dharma alone, and that without any other action on his part the climax of the performance would find him totally naked. But it was not to be; the final curtain had apparently fallen. The show was over.

The lamas tried to persuade us to go with them to the *gompa,* but we had to be getting back. Once we made up our minds to leave it was easy.

About thirty minutes down from Honngoan we stopped at a resting place where we'd taken a lot of pictures earlier on. Sarod and I then had an interesting conversation, which he initiated.

He asked me, without any preamble, if I would send him a copy of my book when it was finished. I had never mentioned I was writing a book; he just assumed it.

The question had a staggering and melancholy effect on me. It was too soon to handle the thought, and it seemed preposterous to me that I'd send a book which probably wouldn't be written anytime soon to a person I was fairly unlikely to locate that far ahead in the future.

"The book's not going to be ready for a while," I apologized in Nepalese. He just nodded his head, and smiled that joyous smile I love so much.

"Very well. After a year or two, then, send it to me. Agreed?"

Agreed, Sarod. And I know you would gladly learn English, just to read that book. . . .

We continued downward at a quick pace, and waded through a herd of cattle. The stones among them were splattered with fresh blood.

"What happened?" I inquired.

"Leeches."

Then we were in the dark dreamy jungle again, now lit with filtered light like a deep aquarium. Hatiya loomed nearer and nearer, and small drops of rain made their way between the leaves.

MAY 9
*Chichila*

It was an infamous morning, pouring in Munche. I hung around until seven, drinking *chang,* eating roasted soybeans and watching Tschering Sherpa Lama complete my protective yantr, which he tied around my neck with prayer and ceremony.

Much good feeling and laughs around the fire. One particularly interesting incident occurred when I decided to acquaint the lama with a couple of exotic taste treats. These were coffee, and cinnamon. I mixed the lama my last cup of Taster's Choice (black) and sprinkled a little bit of the cinnamon on top. God only knows what he thought of it; politeness of course compelled him to utter the requisite *"Mito chha!"*

While Tschering Sherpa Lama was thus savoring the coffee, and everyone else was eating popcorn, I introduced his wife to cinnamon. She liked the smell; so did the lama's son. So I decided, what the heck, and gave the didi my jar of the spice as a gift.

I was sitting there preening my beneficence when the son had the bad manners to ask me, "What do you *use* this on?" A veritable menu of foods came to mind—coffee, hot chocolate, french toast, egg-nog, cakes and cookies, with apples or peanut butter—but, of all of the above, it's possible that the Lama family had, on some past occasion, tasted an apple. Even milk and sugar were absent from their cupboards.

At last the son, having both tasted and smelled the stuff, announced it would be excellent on goat. I'd like to be around the evening they concoct this unthinkable dish.

Finally there was nothing to do for it but pack up as well as I could and emerge from the smoke-filled home onto the unwelcoming path, upon which it was raining like hell.

It was frankly miserable. The ground was mud and slop, puddles ankle-deep, and the pathetic plastic bags I'd tied around over my socks were soon filled with water. Within half an hour I was soaked to the skin from the waist down, panting along, listening to the sound of my breathing echoing in the parka hood. Pressed onward—through the saturated jungle where I'd imagined relaxing to read for a while; up and past Ururus as fresh storm clouds boiled up from the valley below. My feet sloshed with every step, water pouring out of the lace-holes. I felt naked, and painfully aware of the fact that I hadn't a single dry item to put on my feet.

At last the rain abated—a Pyrrhic victory, since I couldn't have gotten any wetter. I took off my hood and in a zombie-like state plowed ahead through deep pools and slippery trails toward Chichila.

No Jew greeted the promised land with more exultation than I, greeting this humble hamlet of three shacks. It took me a long time to manipulate my numbed hands on the straps, buttons, zippers, clasps, safety pins and shoelaces, but at last I was free of my sponge-like wardrobe, watching my sneakers steam by the hearth as the *didi* brought me tea and biscuits.

And then, lo, a miracle! The sky above cleared, powdered Panch Pokhari emerged in the east, and from outside the *didi* cried *"Gaam aunee!"* The sun is out!

This was an hour ago, and since then I've been lying enraptured in the fickle sunshine, trying to believe it's real, and delivering hosanahs to the Lord as my socks dry on the fence.

MAY 14

Got back to Tumlingtar airstrip the morning of the tenth, just in time to hear my flight had been cancelled. The announcement surprised no one but me; it was the sixth day in a row there had been no flight. A party of nineteen people had left on foot, several hours before I arrived, for the fourteen-hour walk to Hille, where one can catch a bus to Dharan, and from there to Itahari, and from Itahari to Kathmandu. The nineteen people had waited four days...I decided to spend the night, and see if they'd send in an unscheduled plane on the eleventh—and, if they didn't, to walk out myself, in *one* day if possible.

The next morning was clear and gorgeous, the Makalu Himal shining long before the sun rose, and only high, puffy clouds in sky. The sun, when it did rise at 6:30, quickly burned off the thick mists rising from the Arun River. At 7, Kathmandu airport radioed Tumlingtar to announce that all flights for the day had been cancelled.

Don't have much to say about May 12, except that it was sort of a blur of the river, Glucose Biscuits, and a seemingly infinite progression of uphill steps, followed by an interminable walk through the fog. Reached Hille after ten hours that pushed me to my limit, and sat on the bus like a zombie. But it all passed quickly... the twelve-hour ride, during a gorgeous day, to Kathmandu, gave me a chance to relax and get my thoughts in order. Also, I finished *Anna Karenin*, an experience which defined the trek, too, in its own obtuse way.

MAY 14

Moments of gazing in wonder over the rows and rows of hills; *dhalbhat* dinners in cavernous rooms lit by single candles; Kitaro on the walkman in the mist; leeches on the sneaker; the lamas that I stayed with, and the kids ... they all become memory. All the colorful journals, filled with revelation and catharsis, all those unrecountable memories.

Everything comes back to memories. Remembering when I first decided to return to Nepal, and why. Remembering America and trying desperately to pull out something that makes up for the rest. Memories on everyone's mind.

On Sunday I went to see Singh the jeweler, to talk about the moonstones I'd brought back from Sri Lanka. We joked for a while. I stole a cigarette; he lit it.

"Oh!" he said, with a sudden intonation of surprise. "Did you hear about Howard?"

"Howard? No, I didn't. Heard he went off with some Japanese climbing expedition. How's he doing?"

"He's dead."

How it happened isn't very clear. He went off by himself, slipped off a ledge and broke his legs, died waiting for help. It's a stunning thing when even a casual friend is killed that way; you find yourself scrutinizing every encounter you'd had, dusting for clues, an understanding of "why him?" All the manufactured reasons. All the memories.

MAY 19

Today was a momentous occasion; Rick and Nancy, my best buddies and housemates, left Nepal this morning to return to the West. This leaves me with an empty house, a throbbing beat of nervous energy, a million disconnected ideas and seven weeks before I am supposed to leave Nepal. The obvious question is, why didn't I give myself more time? I don't know. It's a funny thing. From the moment you leave the States the magnets are at work, subtly exerting their magic to draw you back home. There comes a moment where, borne of preconception and nostalgia, you decide to let them do their work.

MAY 20

The time of the subtle changes, most of them complete but hitherto invisible. Like Rick taking off his shoe the other night and suddenly realizing, with resigned alarm, "Yeah ... my feet ... they didn't use to look this way. They're broader, they've become Nepalese feet." And in his voice that monotonic acceptance of all the subtle yet freakish alterations, most of which you can't even see. Parts of our lives and pieces of our bodies that have evolved to let us survive in

Asia, that will be no more than irritants or curiosities when we return to the West. It's all so hazy, that border between evolution and affectation.

MAY 23

"Sitting some inches off the floor surrounded by flowers?" I'm sitting at the typewriter in my underwear. It's 6:45 A.M., and the reason I got such a late start today is because my bowels think they're at Jericho. Outside the brick and cement and trees are taking on an amber glow; by ten or eleven it'll be hot as hell outside, dusty as an attic and noisy as a camel's ass. Call it burnout. Over the past month my life here has taken some sharp turns, and though I've finally ended up with everything I've wanted (my own house, solitude, money, etc.) I find myself suffering from an intense spiritual restlessness that seems to be taking physical definition in my lower intestines. Been in Nepal for eleven months, still no novel, and something in me is getting tired of being retentive.

In a month or so the monsoon will start, breaking the back of this suffocating dry season. The air will cool; enormous clouds will swarm across the sky; rain will roar down two, three, four times a day, followed by moments of intense sunshine, rainbows, the landscape greening even as the city gutters overflow with mud and shit. Lightning will explode in the night and I'll be lying up in bed at three in the morning wondering how it could ever rain so hard and so long. Those moments make me extremely horny, but the only living things in my flat will be a few gecko lizards and Pablo, the mouse. I'll make do.

America. What can I say? The paradoxes are overwhelming. The difference between us is that, from this distance, everything I hear seems equally profane and shaming, while you, in the belly of the beast, draw fine distinctions to sanctify your own peculiar brand of madness. Those subtleties are lost on me—I can't differentiate between the absurdities of "Where's the beef?" or El Salvador or an art show judged by a dog. It all seems so bloody indulgent to me. I'm ashamed to be an American—Reagan has made me so—but I'm not "speechless with grief." Rather, mad as hell. We *still* represent heroism in the world. If we didn't, you think we could get away with this kind of thing? Heroes sour, but they remain heroes. Saul, Heracles, Howard Hughes, Marlon Brando—myths are hard to kill. The problem with Reagan isn't that he's forgotten the myth. The problem with America isn't that it's forgotten how to be heroic. The problem is that we insist on perpetuating our "rescuers" image in a world that no longer needs or wants to be rescued. Like a senile Quixote, America is like a legend that once drew acclaim from saving a drowning boy, but now flies to the gratuitous service of everyone it sees taking a bath. Yes, I'm as ashamed as you are, easily as puzzled. Puzzled by the Cabbage Patch dolls, the campaign, the bark-o-meter art shows, the supermarkets, the apathy and self-consciousness, the cheap spiritual answers, the big and little bangs. Miss my friends but don't crave my return. If old sack-face is re-elected I'll leave again, not because I don't want to watch but because I *do* ... and you can see it all so much more clearly from a distance.

Steve Durland is wrong when he says we're afraid of dying. Fear of dying is the first step to enlightenment, whether we're talking Buddhism, Judaism or even Russian Orthodoxy (have you read *Anna Karenin?*) Fear of dying is what makes life suddenly precious. The problem is fear of living. Should we be afraid of living? As the Buddha taught, "dissolution is inherent in all formations." Americans are terrified not by death, but by the process of dissolution—everything from running out of milk after the stores are closed to old age to communism to fuel shortages to death. Any society so burning with materialism must by definition be terrified of dissolution, and dissolution is the one fact we cannot alter. How much energy in the States goes toward simply maintaining what is? And is *what is* worth maintaining? We seem to think so, and at any cost. Frankly, I think it's all just a case of too much leisure time.

Enclosed is an article for the *View Point* section of *High Performance*. Hope you can use it.

APRIL 24- MAY 10
*The Arun Valley and environs, Nepal*

## Collecting Blessings

The world is plainly a mess, and sentient beings need all the help we can get. Seeking assistance of any sort I trekked up into the Himalayan foothills in far northeastern Nepal, collecting blessings along the way.

These blessings took four forms:

—Prayer-flags, which I erected on ridges and precipices. These are fine guaze, cotton, silk or even paper flags, block-printed with Buddhist blessings. They are usually flown from long bamboo stalks. Fluttering, they repeatedly send their prayers off to Heaven.

—Circumambulating *mani*-walls. *Mani* means "jewel." A jewel, in this case, is a stone inscribed with a deeply carved blessing, or mantra—usually the familiar *"Om Mandi Padme Huum,"* which means "Endlessly Jewel in the Lotus Vibrating." Long walls of these stones are found through much of northern Nepal. One acquires merit by passing them on the left (i.e., keeping them on one's right or circling them in a clockwise direction).

—Commissioning *yantrs*. A yantr is a blessing from a lama. Each small village has its own lama, or Buddhist interpreter, and all are adept at the art of creating yantrs. A yantr is actually a blessing-made-manifest, meant to be worn around the neck. A lengthy ritual is involved in making each one. Writing in a spiral, the lama first inscribes a prayer on a sheet of rice-paper. He sprinkles it with aromatic powders, folds the blessing into a precise square, wraps it with colored strings and seals the junctures with wax. Finally the lama takes up a *vajra* (thunderbolt) bell and chants protective mantras while waving the whole above a smouldering censor. Once tied on by a lama, a yantr may never touch the ground or be exposed to water. The average fee for a yantr seems to be about four rupees, or twenty cents.

—Praying to God. The method was left to the artist's spontaneous interpretation, and took innumerable forms, which included the following: Silent meditation while listening to Kitaro on a personal stereo; the invention of psalms; ablutions in rivers; compassion toward leeches; giving things away; and conducting a verbal banter with an abstract diety who seemed to combine the best attributes of Zero Mostel, Leo Tolstoy, and Pablo Picasso.

No one, including the artist, was aware that the performance was taking place. The blessings were not counted.

Morning of the eternals: rain and Debussy. Not to mention the fucking mosquitoes. Seven A.M. and gray as a shark outside. I sit here in an antelope-patterned *longi* and nurse my first cup of coffee of the day, feeling the same mixture of ambition and anticipation and dread that greets every one of my days. It's all a bloody mystery to me; what will get done, and when. I only know that the stalemate is over and I'm in a fever of ideas.

I've lived in Nepal for eleven months and eleven days. Pair of elevens: my friend Eric Weiss always thought he'd die at 11:11 one day. I entertain no such traumatic fantasy, but I must admit the day does have the cool, subdued feeling of termination to it. This observation made in spite of my state of relative optimism—things have been going very well. As you may recall I originally came out here to write a novel, an ambition that was repeatedly forestalled and frustrated by my (a) lack of knowledge, (b) lack of understanding, and (c) inability to compose the swarm of ideas that eventually crowded my brain. So for the first year (nearly) of my Asian tenure I gave free rein to my experiential side, hoping that the cacophony of travels and adventures through Nepal, India, Sri Lanka, and the Himalayas would create a situation where everything would somehow fall together of its own volition. Nevertheless, I spent my first year in a rather self-effacing and apologetic mood, "a wallflower at the sacrifice."

Five days ago everything changed. Don't remember exactly what I was doing or how the scene shifted, but the feeling is exactly comparable to that experience of divine revelation one gets when two or three chunks of a jigsaw puzzle suddenly allow themselves to be joined together. Or perhaps I ought to compare the event to an inspiration an artist might receive when working on a collage in which a number of high-potential pieces suddenly arrange their own necessary structure, as if by a movement of their own.

At present I'm confused, blubbering, almost too excited to write. Still ironing out the thousand glitches. Been sketching out characters and scenes, wondering if the idea is too big for one book, trying to stay afloat in the maelstrom by keeping the basic points of integrity solid in my mind. I'm like a horse behind the gate, chafing at the bit—an extremely apt analogy when you consider that the title of the book is *Kanthaka.*

The responsibility that comes with an inspiration is enormous. Teri once said that a book is a gift; now I understand. It's a bizarre mental process, almost like the Jesus-freak alibi: some gifts are so good they've got to be shared. So that's my current mood, in fear and trembling—to share the inspiration I've received—if I'm good enough. The mettle that's been hammered for eleven months is plunged into the water. Now the question is, Where? Leaving Nepal in five weeks with an outline and about fifty pages of sketches and a hundred pages of notes...where?

\*

You postulate that, living in Nepal, I'm "removed" from the election-year scene, Western politics in general. Not so. In fact, I may have a more clear view from this Eastern retreat than do you, the smoke square in your eyes. I think we can agree on one thing: the situation stinks. Reagan is a terror, Khomeini is a panic, Duarte is a puppet, Chernokov is a baby, and virtually all the world leaders are vigorously fist-fucking their constituents. But what strikes me the most is not so much the antics as the audience. I'm talking of America here. Seen from this distance, the mood of America appears to be obscenely bloated and complacent. Our affluence seems almost surrealistic. I cannot help but reflect at this point that the character of Divine in Waters's films seems an almost perfect metaphor: the grotesque, depraved, shit-eating and yet oddly self-satisfied Divine can easily be imagined mashing faces and groins for a shot at the next batch of Cabbage Patch dolls; can be imagined kissing the ground off the airplane from Grenada; can be imagined peering between the buns in obsessive search for "the beef." And not only in these media-inspired fads does America set my teeth on edge. Everything *I* thought was important seems to be shaky and web-like. Does it really matter who wins the convention, even the election? How controversial *is* I.M. Pei? How important *is* Altman's next film or Robert Wilson or anyone's next, last, or future shows? And how important is *Kanthaka*? And where's it all leading? Sometimes I think we're just dressing up the weeds, a "beggars' banquet." Different kinds of beggars out here!

In other words, I dread returning to America, but can't come back until I've risen above that feeling. Well, there's still a lot of *baato* before that bridge.

JUNE 6

Who was talking about the "little fires"? Something from a poem. Hot season in Kathmandu and my spirit's burning like an ulcer. Out beyond my window a field of corn waves and wrinkles in the wind. A year in the Kingdom and everything seems luminous, unreal. The farmer's white shirt, the skittish arcs of birds across the sky, the parade of clouds acting out a tectonic drama. Sometimes, after a smoke, I stand up and the world seems to brown-out into a low hum of tunnel vision...*this* feeling is exactly the opposite. Working at last on my novel I notice that the world-at-large, this bowl in the heart of north central Asia, seems to have roared outward around me, opening up in a thousand directions simultaneously. I can't exist in the shallows anymore. I'm paralysed with joy.

Maybe I'm at last learning patience. It was a very humbling year coming to this point. Things often seemed hopeless. But now, near the end, all the relocations and doubts and processes come ringing together into a matrix, and I understand that without these frustrations there would not have been as good a result. "Some other places were not so good," wrote Hemingway, "or maybe we were not so good when we were in them." Or maybe one is good without meaning to be, and feeling not so good, but once the place becomes history all that hidden, essential good comes rushing out of its own accord, in full possession of its wits, like a bee at daybreak.

Staring out the window at the corn and the plower in the white shirt I can't honestly say that I miss anyone or anything connected with the West. Nevertheless a peculiar gravity seems to be drawing me back; and not without its aura of excitement. Four months from now I'll be back in the States, and a part of me is terribly curious and frightened about it. I'm afraid of sinking myself in an involvement here (with my novel) when I know that in four weeks I'll suffer a break in momentum. What to do? As Calder said, "When you can't sculpt you can always draw." So I'm sketching, getting to know idiosyncracies of my characters and scenes, and trying to convince myself that there will be an end to putting things off.

Living in Kathmandu—with many, many trips to the mountains, India, Sri Lanka, and other nearby locations—has been marvellous. Like a fragrant, gorgeous tree with at least a few rotten fruits on every branch. There are things I've grown to love, and horrible things I would never get used to. Every walk down the streets finds me alternately sucking in the aromas or gritting my teeth and holding my breath. Incense and *sarees* still drive me wild. The butchered goat heads grinning nightmarishly from their fly-blown posts still raise my bile. The gods have gained in status and savagery. The golden eyes of Buddha on the Swayambhu temple still steal my breath away. All the little details have to somehow find their way into *Kanthaka*. Every day I feel like I'm revealing a little too much. I've seen too many people have their heads forced underwater by the weight of their advertised selfexpectations.

Reading Mailer, Salinger, Naipaul, Alexandra David-Neel, and Spider Woman comics, combing the airwaves for Voice of America, pasting together rude collages from the constant spank of native images. You know me. Either riding the horns of the brahmin bulls or hanging on for dear life to the sacred udders, I remain... vaguely comprehensible.

Mozart for the morning. A grayed-in morning to shield us from the eye of the evil pre-monsoon sun.... Typically, I dine on peanut butter, jelly, and coffee from India; like everything else of modern Indian origin the coffee is weak, inadequate in some inexplicable way.

Covered mugs, orange plates, and incense at quarter-to-eight, "There is nothing to investigate."

Like the scatalogical hero of Mailer's *Ancient Evenings*, I force myself or slide through the spectrum of possible worlds. I lied; I'm not ever really lonely, although I sometimes think that I am. During my three-week solo trek up the Arun River, for example, I missed a sharing presence. But some of my finest creative moments occurred in the midst of this narrow solitude. "We must cling to what is difficult," wrote Rilke. He knew that being alone is the most difficult thing of all. But for unobstructed views it is sometimes essential.

I am confronted with the fact that my own departure must soon be at hand. My combination of emotions, if I may be crude, runs the gamut from a prisoner awaiting the sunrise on death row to a virgin bride anticipating her first fuck. Of course, I'm far from a virgin bride, but new destinations always generate a skittish excitement in me. Indonesia is sure to be fascinating; and it also marks the beginning of the process that will carry me back to America this fall.

Looking around, I notice that everything seems ready to leap into a state of transition. I can no longer view my surroundings with a settled eye. The drawing-away has begun, originating from the deepest levels but bubbling to the surface in the form of restlessness...I look outside my window and even the young corn plants seem restless, and the birds arc about restlessly, and the sky, gray as a fender and perched just above the monsoon, fills me with melancholy and restless apprehension. I worry my nails. Nine in the morning and I've been up for hours, whistling Rachmaninoff but listening to Bach (!). But now the Bach has ended, and in an attempt to pull myself into the present I pop *West Meets East* (Menuhin/Shankar) into the deck.

What am I afraid of? I feel like the host of some kind of beautiful pregnancy, but have no idea when the novel will be born. I can't determine if laziness or a surfeit of excitement is holding me back. This may seem odd, but writing those words it occurs to me that I might try to take a Tantric attitude toward it—that is, cultivate a relaxed but dynamic state in which my energies build, patiently, relentlessly, culminating in something very close to fire.

Thanks for sharing this morning with me. "Be like the sun at mid-day."

Listening to *Parkening Plays Bach* in my current mood is like trying to read Walt Whitman on a roller-coaster. Don't ask me why I'm jumping out of my skin; maybe the fact that I'm leaving Nepal three weeks from tomorrow has something to do with it. And then again, you ought to be forewarned that the current interpretation of "jumping out of my skin" has little or no relation to the Jeffish histrionics you are probably picturing in your mind. The fact is that I've calmed down somehow, somewhat, compared to the way I was a year ago. A year in Asia has its effect—or *affect*, as it will no doubt seem when I return to the States. Imagine the following dialog:

"Hey, Jeff?!"

" हजुर ?"

The monsoon is in full swing. Getting around is miserable, but the flowers and cloudscapes more than make up for it. More time spent indoors than usual, although I'm out to swim (at the Hotel Annapurna) every afternoon. This solitary final act, like most soliloquies, contains a fair share of self-analysis. Actually, that's the worst word I could have used; let me say self-appraisement. Naturally this is an ongoing process through one's life, but there is a remarkable difference. In the West this introspection takes place under the eye of a competitive and all-consuming lifestyle; here in Nepal one works beneath the serene and charming regard of Buddha. Instead of a subaudible "more... more... more," one hears the placid "fine... fine... fine." Different kinds of encouragement, I guess. Even swimming is different somehow. When I jump into the pool at about two or three I see the upcoming laps as a relaxed, even yogic meditation. To put it yet another way—in the West I'd be thinking about how my bathing suit looked on me, in the East I'm more concerned with the fit of my *chakras*.

JUNE 13

Woke up this morning feeling like something scraped off the tail of a sacred cow. And why not? Up 'til the wee hours imbibing forbidden pleasures... and my partying neighbors making such a ruckus that I was forced to take a Valium for dessert. I peeled myself off the mattress this morning, already a spent man, and my first thought of the day, inevitably, was the countdown: three weeks from today (in theory at least) I am off, gone for temporary good from my favorite live-in sewer-cum-stable; gone from the obscured shadows of the world's sharpest mountains; gone from the twenty-rupee feasts and thirty cent wedges of apple and chocolate and banana cream pie; gone from the oozing, sopping rice paddies and the puddinged monsoon streets, the infernal, eternally busted telephones, Yak cigarettes, *topis*, the Manangi money changers, the corner butcher haking away at the water-buffalo skulls; gone from the pacific eyes of the Buddha and the blunt Shiva lingams and the brass bells surrounding shrines to the elephant god Ganesh... hey... so long! So I sat up with "matter" running from both eyes and staggered to the bathroom to regard, with all requisite fear and loathing, the countenance you so diplomatically described as "maturing"... try as I might I could not wash off the face, so I contented myself with a cup of coffee and bowl of curd, and installed myself at the desk to better contemplate both the unimaginable length and discombobulating brevity of Three More Weeks.

Good morning, and welcome to "Mister Raja's Neighborhood." Yes...that animal you see outside the window is a cow...cows are sacred here in Mr. Raja's town, which means that if you kill one in a traffic accident you go to jail for life...what's that, Amy? What happens if you hit a *person*? Oh, don't be silly. Why, you just keep driving just as fast as you can, and don't look back... and this—quiet, children—this is a dog...do you see what he's doing? Yes! He's lapping up the poop that that little boy just shat onto the street, and now...do you see? That's right, he's licking the little boy clean! So you can see, Susie, how very important dogs are to help keep Kathmandu clean and tidy...Horace, what other helpful or friendly animals can you spot? Very good! Yes, that's a water-buffalo at the corner, but I'm surprised you recognized it! After all, it *is* hacked to pieces, and all the hair has been boiled off...that's right, Julie, that's the same water buffalo that was tied up outside the shop last night...that's why the meat is still steaming!

It's 7 A.M. and some blue's breaking through the sky. A good sign, as the monsoon is in full swing and this blue omen portends no rain for at least the next few hours. I love the monsoon for the cloudscapes and clarity of the air, but my God, the streets—it's a nightmare to get around. Needless to say I'm a slave to my lists and errands these days. The countdown continues. Tho' the frantic hounds are at bay there will come a time, very soon, when my entire life will be little more than a physical and spiritual preparation for departure.

Work on the writing has reached an interesting level, sort of a semi-static dynamic. The vortex of ideas and stimulations that have been brewing in my mind during my tenure here finally began a ballet of bonding...a tantric dance of conjugal ecstasy. By the time another week had passed I had the preliminary outline on paper and the characters (there are five main ones) sketched out in detail. Lots of research followed, since much of the novel has to do with Buddhist and Hindu mythology, and involves various mythic sites scattered around the Kathmandu Valley. Locations in the Himalayas and in India as well...not to mention the Celestial Kingdom. Some questions: Where does a man end and a god begin? Is there any noticeable difference between a person who is genuinely naive and one who is utterly confused? How did it feel to be a horse? What was Buddha's favorite between-meal snack? Ah, slowly, it comes together. But sadly and inevitably my heart is not into writing right now. I'm restless and half-mad at the thought of my imminent departure, and there seem to be a thousand little things to do and to consider prior to my flight. So as I see it, I'll slate January-May of 1985 for the writing of *Kanthaka*. Anyone who heard me bitterly complaining eighteen months ago that I "must write my novel in Nepal" will be uproariously amused by my current anthem, which goes, "I'm going to have to try to write my novel in America." Can't you just

see it ... the human squash-ball, swatting himself between the perpendiculari-
ties of East and West, ever in motion, never able to stay still long enough to get
his own bearings. I loathe this current of distraction in myself.

A final thought about this novel business, which is that it seems to be
imitating by accident or design the birth-process of a homo sapiens; they say it
actually takes a babe eighteen months to be born; that the first nine womb-
months are followed by an equally long post-womb period where the bones
harden, the optic mechanisms focus, the palate finds its possibilities. So let's
say that *Kanthaka*, having finally popped out from the darker recesses, has to
learn to survive in my mind before it gets onto paper.

Hanging out alone, mostly, although there have been a few encounters with interesting transients—"ghosts," as I call them. But nothing holds my interest for very long these days. Reading a lot, writing some, making an infinity of lists and walking the streets with the metal tip of my umbrella striking the pavement, a Yak dangling from my lower lip. Trying to notice things I haven't noticed properly before. Broadening my knowledge about the seamier side.

I paid a visit to the jail a couple of days ago and found it a surprisingly convivial place. There are three Americans in now: a record. It was weird to see these people, whom I'd recognized from around Thamel, with the sad, lost look in their eyes, through the thin iron bars...a place I'll never be. But the final two scenes of *Kanthaka* take place in the Dillibazar prison, so I kept my eyes open and tried to project my character Saury into that crowded, non-libidinal place. It'll fly.

Deepak, the mail clerk at American Express, left this morning for Europe, then he's off to Australia. I took him out to dinner at San Francisco Pizza and we had a terrific discussion about development, the West, Judaism, and mail forwarding. Gave him that green polo shirt that Rick had tried out, as well as my suitcase. Everybody a Winner as the sahibs leave town...well, almost everybody: The Beggar with the Longest Arms in the World ("Saaaaab... Saaaaab...") has changed his location. He has now planted himself, night-marishly, as a human roadblock just in front of the entrance to Narayan's Pie Shop. Imagine my surprise as, driven by my addiction to pie and ice cream, I approached the cafe at 10 P.M. to be confronted by that unwelcoming dirge... "Saaaab..." "Oh, God," I couldn't help saying, "what are *you* doing *here*?"

It's almost ten in the morning. Tchaikovsky's Piano Concerto no. 1 is rustling from the stereo behind me while just ahead, right outside my window, the day's first monsoon downpour is abating to a trickle. There is an onion on my desk: A Dutch woman named Sophie told me that the best cure for a head cold is to sniff a halved onion once or twice every fifteen minutes. Well, if I wasn't the sort of guy who'll try anything at least once I guess I wouldn't be sitting here right now, deep in the mystic muck of Kathmandu, watching sparrows jitt between the silver cornstalks and listening to the howl of dogs being lamed by rickshaws... I've lived in Nepal for 370 days and if an onion can cure me, I'll surround myself with *yo kasimko* legumes, sleep with onions, tie a halved onion like a mask around my face as I type.

But I think it's more than an ordinary cold. One year and four days in The

World's Only Hindoo Kingdom and some mechanism in me—the overdrive that's been grinding my physiology uphill these past Asian months—knows that I'll soon be shifting to second. According to plan—the exasperating plan—I've got twelve more days in this country, and then set off on a Hatter's ride of plane flights which should put me in Jakarta by the 6th of July. I'll be in Java when you receive this, perhaps... the Equator in July. Could there be a worse time to have a cold? My defenses are down, and everything I'm needing to get me through these frenetic final weeks—from cocaine to pick-ups to valiums to my daily swim—is contributing to the fog that's clouding my head. Horny but exhausted, driven but cynical, committed yet faithless, I roll and stumble through my final week-and-a-half in the place I labored seventeen months to be, and juggle the apple, cabbage, and sword from the spastic midst of the dance. Sound like the Jeff you used to know? Only on paper... looking back on the mess that the typewriter and I have conspired to create just now, I realize that my problems may be quite simply stated after all: I'm dying to get out of here, and I cannot bear the thought of leaving.

*

Act Two: 10:30. Jarre's *Oxygene* on the deck, like a thousand singing penguins. After I changed the tape I stood up and stared, open-mouthed, through my window and across the fields at the women passing bricks hand-to-hand on a nearby roof. A third of Kathmandu is under construction, and the city's changed more in the last six months than in the whole five years since my previous visit. For the worse, I add, sourly, inevitably. And in another five years, will I even recognize this place?

Day before yesterday I rode home on my Hero bicycle and, as I turned off the main street onto the dirt path leading to my house, I saw the neighbor's gardeners fencing the entire roadway with fresh barbed wire. I stopped my bike.

"What are you doing?!?"

"Wire, *sahib*."

"Yes, thanks, I can see that. It's horrible. Why are you putting it up?"

"We must plant flowers here."

"I don't make the connection."

"The goats will come, and eat the flowers."

Did I tell you that a goat actually came into my house? There I was, haplessly typing, when I heard the unmistakably report of cloven hooves behind me.... The goat stood naively in the spare room, absently chewing Ronald Reagan's face off the front page of an *International Herald Tribune*. I tried to lure him outside with a ripe Roma tomato, but after following me halfway down the steps he bolted up into the house again, and I followed in hot pursuit, finally substituting the proverbial stick for the proverbial carrot.

Okay, so the goats are a problem—but they've been here for hundreds of years, and there are still plenty of flowers in the Valley. Oh, shit, listen to the Jew babbling up his racial phobia... An upcoming letter-to-the-editor of the *Rising Nepal* will show you the extent of my obsession.

The sky is turning gray as a hippo's ass, and it's about to rain for the first time in ten minutes. The monsoon is all right, but it would be lovely without the taxis and motorcycles that careen through the silvery alleys and throw waves of hookworm-infested muck onto my legs. Ah, it's tough to be a Buddhist. But I've got to keep trying. Those deep breaths are all that keep me from yanking open the taxi doors, hauling out the vacant-skulled drivers and introducing them, face-first, to the nearest mountain of goatshit. But *calme-toi*; all is beneficence; remember the Eightfold Path.

I'm clearly out of control with this letter. Time for another hit of Onion.

JUNE 26

Leaving Nepal, lovely, stinky, soaking-wet Nepal, Nepal of my dreams for so many months. Nepal of so many restless afternoons. Nepal of butchered smoke and incense alleyways and paddies and sarees and stool-samples; Nepal like all the best parts of a woman, and that is all of them; Nepal of the lingam and yoni and eternal asshole; Nepal in the mist, in the freezing cold winter months; Nepal beneath the rains, even last night, of a low and perpetual monsoon, the streets ankle-deep, the bastard taxis throwing up walls of water, the tethered *baishi* awaiting the blade, the squatting *bahini* awaiting the dog who will lick her clean afterwards; Nepal of the dancing gods, the glass-bead thickets, the lepers and worms and temple-struts carved with scenes of Tantric sex; leaving Nepal after one year and three weeks, bound for no place any less beautiful and strange.

# The RISING NEPAL

APRIL 21 1984   SATURDAY

## Letters

# Barbed Wire Progress

During recent trips around the Kathmandu Valley I have been disheartened to see a new addition to the landscape. From Changu Narayan to Nagarkot, out towards Bhaktapur and up to Patan, barbed wire is throwing its ugly vines everywhere. The galvanized tendrils run over hill and down dale, and are beginning to make Kathmandu's pastoral suburbs look like prison camps.

Far from me to question the utility of barbed wire, or of any of these heavy-gauge fencings that have so suddenly laced the country. I am sure that wire is essential in a place like Chitwan, where an ecosystem must be protected, or as a means of holding together laboriously collected stone dams. But I must question the motives of the department responsible for lining the Nagarkot — Bhaktapur road with barbs. Strung across ravines and along impossibly steep ridges, the frightful fencing will not arrest a bus plunging over into the abyss — nor will it do anything but shred the hapless victim who might stumble (or be pushed) off the road and into its clutches. In some places the barbed wire is strung pell-mell over roads and creeks, apparently because it was too much trouble to interrupt the happily spinning spools long enough to end one fence and begin another.

The wire demands immediate removal on the bare grounds of ugliness and uselessness, but there is also something genuinely alarming about it. The malignant strands are being used as clotheslines all along their run. You don't have to be an "Appropriate Technologies" researcher to realize that hanging laundry over barbed wire will lead to ruined clothes and higher clothing bills. What's more, the wire will eventually begin to corrode and rust, and the barbs — which are now merely dangerous — will become potentially lethal opportunities for village children to contract tetanus and blood poisoning. And while we're on the subject of children, let's take the briefest moment to speculate about the psychological effects of having your rural environment festooned overnight with meter after meter of metal thorns. Aren't you glad you didn't grow up with barbed wire around **your** house?

**Jeff Greenwald**

Chhetrapatti
Kathmandu.

The end of an era always has a sense of anti-climax about it; you know how long I waited and how hard I labored to get here. And maybe you know how much ambition accompanied me. I've accomplished a hell of a lot less and a hell of a lot more than I set out to. I've achieved some kind of potency, but even that word contains its own betrayal: the seed of the word "potential." What I had hoped for was not just the capacity, but for a massive ejaculation of some sort—something to bind word and image, personality and vocation.

Yes, the adventures out here have been fantastic, and there's no end in sight. Leaving in another week for an *Islands* assignment in Indonesia, then off to meet Teri in Japan. But it's getting to be a thin line between adventure and distraction. It's not as if you have to explore the world with a compass and a machete anymore. One sets off for the volcanic islands and wonders how the food will be, how the women will be, how the coffee will be, how the mosquitoes will be. I'm getting tired of it, but at this point I don't think I have the energy to go any deeper. There will be an end to it in the fall. I only hope that all roads lead to *Kanthaka,* and that the immense fear that's slowly digesting my inspiration will recede once I sit down with the completed outline and a blood-vow.

You say, "I have been learning more about fear lately." I suppose that statement was a response to the postcard I sent you, of *Kal Bhairab,* God of Terror. I am now sending you a card of Buddha, which has replaced the one of David Smith on my wall. The *mudra,* or pose, is called "Subduing Mara." During the weeks he single-mindedly meditated toward enlightenment, Siddhartha was assailed by the underworld king Mara, who bedeviled him with every variety of temptation and fear, but to no avail. Finally Mara confronted the would-be Buddha personally and demanded, "What gives you the right, who gives you the license, to claim this position for yourself?" In response, and without moving his left hand from his lap, Siddhartha reached down with his right and touched the Earth.

Think of yourself as sitting in that flat left palm. It never trembles.

Jazz and a slight headache at 11:30 P.M. With only a couple of days left in Nepal it's necessary to burn a little midnight oil. And I definitely want to write you before I leave—you were the first person I wrote to from Nepal, and will be the second to last. You can imagine the various traumas assailing me as I prepare to empty my home, eat my farewell dinners and pack my bags. It's difficult, and even under the best of circumstances I think I'd feel a little tested by the process. But the past few days have not witnessed the best of circumstances. Health sort of down; some anonymous, spacy malaise which could be anything from tension to worms to paratyphoid; though I feel a lot of it's emotional. General lassitude and introspection on the eve of departure. I'm *tearing* myself away—is this trip necessary? Then there's the fact that these final few weeks I've been meeting some very interesting people, making some good new friends, realizing another dimension of this remarkable community's potential. Had my first dinner with a group of contemporary, highly educated Nepalese—men and women—and was fascinated by what I've been missing. Don't it just always happen this way?

Last Saturday—the 30th of June—a friend and I went up the Valley rim to a beautiful ridge and ate tabs of the finest LSD I've ever tasted. It was a stunning, gorgeous afternoon; both of us well aware that we were at a sort of apex in our lives, and that—geographically, at least—we had "arrived" at the perfect Spot. I don't think I've ever felt more relaxed or more lucky. When it got late, and the evening monsoon clouds filled the valley like a school of whales, we climbed down to our ridiculous little car. The whole village was massed around it, just admiring it with wonder; and we had to admire it, too. We climbed in, put a Grateful Dead tape on the deck and cruised home through Chobar Gorge, as sons and fathers with white teeth strolled along the roadside and the cement factory filled the Valley with death-gray smoke. But we were very alive. We just went home and danced, danced, danced, then drank beer and danced some more. That was the last time I felt good enough to dance.

The grass is always greenest just before it disappears under the mower, and Nepal has never looked better. Even the slop in the rained-out road is endearing. Everywhere I look I see tableaux, perfect little allegories of everything I've seen before. The rickshaws grouped around the Chhetripaati bandstand at 11 P.M., drivers sprawled sleeping across the seats and under their umbrellas; the mud-sparrows' nest on the shelf in the pharmacy; the corner flashlight-repairmen and umbrella-fixers and disposable-lighter refilling stands and sunglass salesmen; the traffic cops dancing around on their pedestals with impotent histrionics; the huge fruitbats hanging from the trees in front of the Royal Palace. Those bats had a great effect on me last July, and as I ride up Thamel avenue I can always find one or two groups of tourists standing agape on the opposite sidewalk, pointing in disbelief to the hanging nocturnals.

The Fourth of July bash at the American Compound, tomorrow, seems more than ever like a sick and ugly party for sick and ugly people—"Because of a large expected turnout, we ask that you do not bring your Nepali friends along"—it's great to be an American. Everything around me seems ready to raise itself to its highest level of poignancy or beauty or filth or absurdity, seems ready to burn itself into my brain for the benefit of these final days here. Be certain my head is spinning.

And in the center of it all, like a scorching beacon of pain and pride and necessity, *Kanthaka* rears up and snorts furiously, demanding everything and wondering who could possibly be so awkward with the reins.

Packed are the statues and glass beads and wooden stamps. Packed the plates and cutting boards, the T-shirts, the King and Queen buttons. The dusty straw mats are rolled up and silverfish scurry away from the bare spaces where posters and collages hung. A life comes down from the shelves and walls and wonders where next, and why. And the time flies by. How I've watched it go; how lean and pale I've become here, searching so dizzily for gold, encouragement, inspiration. How giddy I've become without passion. How naked I feel as I prepare to leave. How tightly it's all packed.

JULY 4-5

Twenty past eleven, the walls empty, the last remaining flakes of coke off the mirror, a cigarette and a half and *Avalon* to get me through this next-to-last evening in Nepal. The desk, floors, shelves in a turmoil of departure, serving up the final gasps and gimmicks of what's been one hell of a year. So many memories for one year. But listen: time is a sugar-coated digestive pill; a broad-spectrum anthelminic; a marble of hashish. What do I have to show for it, except a few more ribs?

Not spending much time looking back. There are more dangerous thoughts: mostly that I'm leaving too soon, too close to the brink of something that might only be able to happen here. In order to convince myself to leave it's been necessary to invest in a psychological return ticket. "You can always come back," said Elliot Marseille, as we sat on the prayer-flag hill at Pharphing and watched the current of prayers ripple, shimmering, up from the lines of galloping flags...both of us realizing: there is nothing/more than this. Nothing more than the crowd of flags like a herd in the wind. Nothing more than the drone from the halls of the Buddhist nunnery below us. Nothing more than the play of light and shadow across Kathmandu Valley. This was the most beautiful spot on earth once; it's changing fast, but has not lost its ability to surprise and inspire me, or move me to tears of rage and frustration. I love Nepal.

It's a very private thing, this leaving. You can't know what it's been like for me out here. A few loose descriptions on paper, like a scratching from some doorway down the hall. Sometimes I walk along the street and just by keeping my eyes open learn everything I'll ever need to know about integrity and innocence. Life in the Zone of Peace. You really must pass a full year to have some notion. And even at that rate, I'm leaving too soon.

Private, but you've been with me much of the time. A vacant spot of always frustrated curiosity in my head, saying, "What if Jekel..." So mysterious a countenance, yours, that even during the past week's orgy of shopping and clutching at objective links for self and friends (e.g., "souvenirs") I have not laid eyes on one item of any sort that would seem an appropriate gift to bring you from this place. Maybe that's why our dialog has endured on the level it has: there's zero link between my relationship with you and my relationship with this place. I'd really like to bring you something precious, but it could be no better than an allegory. Like bringing back a rock from the Moon—but even those had contagious excitement.

Have I succeeded at all with this letter of conveying a shadow of the light, a whisper of the explosion?

*

Ah, the gentleness of this place. The scene on Thamel avenue today: a *very* pretty pale-brown cow standing on the sidewalk, between a cigarette stand and an umbrella repairman, her head lifted straight up, perpendicular with the ground, while a ten-year-old boy heading home from school stood there, reaching up and scratching the animal's neck. Meanwhile all the tourists pointing to the fruit-bats hanging in the trees. The smell of bat shit and garbage and day-old murk, literally Another Shitty Day in Paradise. Shangri-la's getting wasted, but you can still stand on the street corner in Kathmandu and scratch her heavy velvet throat.

On Saturday I clearly understood that Art has got to be either political or holy. There's nothing else but compulsion and self-indulgence. The book I write will have to be holy first, political second. I mean what I say about "making the world safe for enlightenment." Heads will roll; Kali will dance with the garland of disembodied hands bleeding around her waist. Some people will faint and some will froth at the mouth. Some will waste away in the Dillibazar prison, its gate bordered by artful crayoned flowers. Some will throw their arms up and try to catch the lightning. Some will burrow underground. I just hope I can keep my pencils sharp. "And write about it afterwards," said Hemingway, "but not too damn long afterwards."

The sweaty room at quarter-to-one. Lots of things making noise outside. Voices out on the path. My body is coated with a fine film of sweat, my pulse is racing, my knuckles are stiff. Something's coming down outside; it could only be rain. Rain on the cornstalks. Some things sure do grow up fast. Well, we can't all be vegetables.

Let me leave you for now in the rain.

This afternoon I took a last, soft journey to Pashupatinath temple, which is built around the holy Bagmati River. Watched the monkeys and tourists for a spell, then wandered out the trails into a small woods behind the temple complex. Found a small, circus-like shrine for Ganesh, the god of auspicious beginnings, covered with *tika* powder and pasteled-out in the fading evening light. I left a coin in the curl of his trunk and rang rang rang the bells. Where does one thing end and another begin? "See you in March?" I tell/ask my friends. No one knows why I'm leaving. But I'm used to this kind of useless uprooting—it always has its use, after all, in the end.

## ABOUT THE AUTHOR

JEFF GREENWALD was born in the Bronx, New York City. He has traveled extensively through Europe and Asia, working as a photographer, writer, and graphic artist. In addition, Mr. Greenwald has developed educational programs and exhibits for the San Francisco Exploratorium and Santa Barbara Museum of Art and worked with refugees on the Thai-Cambodian border. He has been a magazine and newspaper editor (*eye, Art-Life,* and the *Santa Barbara News & Review*), and his articles have appeared in a wide variety of national and international publications.

*Mister Raja's Neighborhood,* the intimate record of a year in Asia, is Mr. Greenwald's first book.